# Open Your Ears to Love

*by*

## Bettine Clemen

*May your life be filled with love*

*f Bettine*

The Hovenden Press
Minneapolis, Minnesota
USA

Compiled and edited by Suzanne Ford and Peter Longley
Cover concept and design by Anthony J.W. Benson and Mori Studio
Interior design by Mori Studio
Cover photograph by Anthony J.W. Benson
Back cover photograph by Erica Mueller
Back cover portrait photograph by Glamour Shots
Interior biography portrait by Erica Mueller

Published by The Hovenden Press
P.O. Box 1426, Minnetonka, Minnesota 55345 USA

Manufactured by Geehan Graphics, Inc
7108 Ohms Lane, Edina, Minnesota 55439

ISBN: 0-9666770-1-3

Library of Congress Catalog Card Number: 98-88907

Clemen, Bettine
Open Your Ears to Love/Bettine Clemen – 1st Hovenden Press ed.
p. cm.
ISBN: 0-9666770-1-3
1. Title - Autobiography

First The Hovenden Press. Edition 1999

Printed in the United States of America
03  02  01  00  99   9  8  7  6  5  4  3  2  1

*Dedicated*
*to*
*David*


*"Life is a song*
*for the heart that is free."*

# Table of Contents

# Acknowledgments

As this book is a sharing of my life's journey, I feel deep appreciation and gratitude to the countless people, who have inspired me and who enriched my life through their presence. There are too many to mention them all by name, but I would like to thank my husband, Peter Longley, the author of *Two Thousand Years Later* and *The Magdala Trilogy*, for his encouragement and ceaseless work in assisting me in shaping this book. He was instrumental in bringing a series of travel essays into a cohesive whole. Likewise, I am indebted to my good friend and writer Suzanne Ford for her editorial work and collaboration in recording my stories. Without Suzanne's and Peter's input *Open Your Ears to Love* would never have become the inspirational tool that I hope it can now become.

I have been blessed to have met and encountered so many wonderful people who have contributed to my life experience. I remember with gratitude my parents, Wolfgang and Ursula Clemen who introduced me to the joys of nature and the sound of music, and whose qualities I came to appreciate more and more as I traveled on my independent path. Both of my brothers, Christian and Harald helped me to learn to stand up for myself in earliest childhood, and later, especially after the death of my parents, I felt our loving bond as a strong presence in my life.

My sincere thanks go to all my music teachers, flute professors and mentors, starting with my first recorder instructor in my home village in Southern Germany and my music teacher in high school, Mr. Wolfgang Bachleitner. I fell in love with him and with the world of music that he presented to us in such an exciting way, and even though I had already set my mind to be a flutist at age six, it was Wolfgang Bachleitner who helped me to dedicate myself completely to the study of music at the Academy. All my formative flute teachers need to be mentioned here and my deepest thanks go to them for all that they passed along to me even in my very lazy and unfocused times: Walther Theurer at the Munich Academy with his life long experience at the Munich National Opera; Aurele Nicolet, who probably was my toughest teacher, but also one of my best (when I auditioned for him, he said: "It sounds very nice, but everything is wrong!"); Peter-Lukas Graf, whose incredible musicality and sensitivity is still an example for me today. Julius Baker taught me a lot about always putting the music first, as did Marcel Moyse. Finally, there was James Galway, whose master classes inspired me with new ideas on sound and energy in music.

I am deeply grateful to many spiritual guides and Masters for their insights and patience, particularly to the Living ECK Masters from Paul Twitchell to Harold Klemp, who helped me explore the wonders of the inner and outer worlds of light and sound. I am also grateful for the silent divine love that I have experienced in the presence of Mother Meera.

My thanks also go to all of those whom I met by chance, but who ignited a spiritual response within me and through that "opened my ears to love." In particular among them are Harold Solmssen, my dear spiritual friend and mentor; Dr. Kenneth Ring, who helped me understand and appreciate my near-death experience; Elleva Joy McDonald, who introduced me to 'Avatar'; and all the characters whom I have recorded in this book... people from all races and nationalities from around the world along with countless others, whom I have not recorded, but who remain just as close to my heart. We are all one in our interconnectedness in spirit.

Growth has also come to me in many other ways. The love and joy that I have encountered in animals and the natural world has been every bit as important in my spiritual journey as the shared compassion of humanity. I remember with particular joy the lessons I learned and the love that I shared with the ponies and horses of my childhood, Ilse and Svadi in particular. I thank the camels, penguins, kangaroos, koalas, donkeys, dogs, birds and dolphins that populate the pages of this book, along with the countless life forms that I have failed to mention, for the unconditional love that they have shown. I offer special thanks to my stuffed companions who have traveled the world with me, the many teddy bears and other creatures whom you will also meet in the pages of this book—they are important, too.

There are many others whom I want to acknowledge. They include my publicist Anthony Benson who has been instrumental in helping me launch *Open Your Ears to Love*; a young boy named David who is the inspiration for this story; and the musicians with whom I share my professional career and in particular my guitar partners Richard Patterson and Barbara Polasek; harpists Kim Robertson and Andrea Stern, along with concert pianists Lorin Hollander and Nana Muhkadze. I thank the conductors of the orchestras in which I have played... the officers, staff and crew of the many ships on which I have sailed... the loved ones with whom I have shared a part of my life—all of them are of equal importance.

After I started to write this book, I discovered the tools of 'Avatar.' In many ways, these have confirmed, expanded and enriched my life's journey, and for that I will forever be grateful. 'Avatar' gave me my concluding message, which is so well expressed by Harry Palmer, the author of the 'Avatar' materials, whose quote can be found at the end of the Epilogue.

*Bettine Clemen*
*October, 1998*

# Preface

In my early childhood years, I had three memorable dreams: the first one was about traveling and exploring the whole world, the second was about playing music, in particular the flute, and the third was about experiencing tangible love. I daydreamed for hours on end sitting on the hard benches in the elementary school of my small Bavarian village. Too many times, the harsh voice of my German first-grade teacher brutally interrupted my journeys and I was jolted back into the reality of that dark and sinister schoolroom. Daydreaming was definitely not "hip" in those days in Bavaria. But, I continued to live in my own wonderful world, and in my imagination I traveled to distant lands and even out into the cosmos just as had been promised in that first dream.

Music and my ponies became a healing sanctuary for me even as a small girl. Whenever there were problems with my two older brothers, (and with two brothers there were a lot of fights and conflicts,) I either went to my pony and told him everything and then cried into his mane, or I took out my recorders and played all my feelings into those small flutes until I would feel better. I remember clearly the effects of my self-made music and love therapy. The love bond between my pony and me made me forget all my troubles instantly, and the music always lifted me into a much more joyful state. These early childhood discoveries and experiences became a basis for my life's journey that continued to soar with the power of music, love and travel. My dream was strong enough to be fulfilled, and even though there was much discouragement along the way, my strong desire to eventually become a professional flutist and travel the world manifested in a wondrous way.

One of the questions most asked of me at the end of any performance is "What is the difference between a 'Flutist,' a 'Flautist' and a 'Flautiste?'" My answer has always been the same—"The difference lies in the salary." There are no hard and fast guide lines although preferences in this matter vary slightly around the world. For this reason in the pages of this book you will find 'Flutist' and 'Flautist' are used indiscriminately.

Music, being the universal language of the world, opened doors for me to connect with thousands of people from different continents, cultures and races. Music and sound opened the doors also to my inner worlds and helped me to discover the spiritual dimension that is the creating essence for all of our experiences. Through music I found my real self. I believe that there are many ways to the truth and that in the end it will always be "our truth" and "our way." It simply can't be the same for everybody and yet every living being is of the same essence. Some connect with this life force through nature, others through music or through religious practices, or just through being present in every moment.

For me, music has been a guiding force in my life and I want to share some of my most treasured experiences in this book. One can only experience the reality of music and love. That experience creates energy that has the power to touch our innermost being. It uplifts us; can heal us; transform us; soothe our emotions; illuminate us, and raise us into a different state of consciousness. I felt that stories would express the inner music of my life better than a theory book on decibels. My greatest joy lies in sharing music and love with people, animals, and plants. We are all inter-connected and share the vibration of the sound current.

Historically, we can encounter a profound understanding and awareness of the secret power of music. This knowledge was often expressed in the philosophies of ancient times. The Chinese philosophy of the Tao; Isis and Osiris in ancient Egypt; Plato and Pythagoras in classical Greece, and Persian Sufis all have given evidence of their integration of music as a healing force. Music was recognized as a tangible power, which could change people for better or for worse.

Many religions talk about the "word" as the beginning of creation. Although they used different names they were referring to the same universal vibratory energy that was the "Music of the Spheres" to the

Pythagoreans of Greece, the celestial energies of perfect harmony to the ancient Chinese, the words of their Gods to the Egyptians, the Shabda, or Nada Brahma in ancient India and the sound current to some spiritual teachings. This inner music, most often shut off by the rush of our thoughts and the noise of our world, can re-link us with that divine origin of all life.

In our times, as stress increases and people everywhere are faced with enormous challenges and demands, music has been rediscovered as a wonderful source for healing mankind's physical, emotional and mental illnesses. This has happened together with an accelerated spiritual awakening, that seems to be taking place all over the world.

Everything is in a state of change. All the old ways of thinking are challenged and new paradigms are opening people's minds. There seems to be a speeding up of encounters with like-minded people all over the planet. An awakening is taking place. It is an awakening of our soul energy... a growing awareness in many... an awareness that we are each a song, a note of God—we are here to express our spiritual essence.

I have been so fortunate in my profession as a concert flutist to be able to travel around the world many times. My adventures and experiences of all kinds have one common denominator: they all strengthened the knowingness in me that all life is a growing spiritual awareness. The thousands of people I have met on my tours, along with the animals and the plants all taught me something very valuable about our common awareness. They taught me to listen more, to open my heart and to open my ears to love.

And so, this book is a sharing of all these experiences that sparkle in my heart now as jewels, which have helped me to appreciate divinity.

In my profession as a solo flutist I get many letters. People often express gratitude and enthusiasm for the music, but some express envy at all the traveling that I get to do. They write things like this: 'If we could only travel as much as you do, if we could travel around the world all the time, then maybe we would have all these exciting spiritual experiences.' But, such experiences have nothing to do with traveling, although sometimes travel can open our eyes and ears. Spiritual experiences have much more to do with the rediscovery that we all are "Divine" energy. We are that which runs our physical bodies, and we are that which never dies.

Of all the letters that I have received, however, my favorite came from an eight-year-old boy who wrote to me… 'Dear Bettine… Your concert was one of the best concerts I never went to. I loved the music; and by the way, how much money do you make playing those flutes, and do you have any better dresses? Love David.' This was then followed with a post scriptum—'PS: Life is a song for the heart that is free.' That is all I can wish for anyone, that our lives could be songs expressing the freedom of our hearts.

We can be both the conductor and the players of this symphony, the song that we call our life. We can be aware of being that creative energy that crafts and plays our life's music. We are all the sounds, melodies, harmonies and rhythms in that music. The fullness of all there is can be expressed in every individual life. And life can be a song… a symphony of love.

Open your ears to love.

*Open Your Ears to Love*

*Out of stillness in the morning,*
*Sounds are rising to embrace you.*
*Out of darkness in the night time,*
*Lights are flowing to ignite you.*
*Let them lift you into heavens.*
*Open your ears to love!*

*From the oceans that are swirling,*
*Whales and Dophins come to guide you,*
*From the forests that are breathing,*
*Eagles soon will soar to wake you.*
*Follow now the call of Spirit,*
*Open your ears to love!*

*–Bettine*

# Chapter One

# Animal Gifts

At age six, I wrote a very sincere letter to Santa Claus: "Please bring one horse with a saddle and stirrups," it said in crooked German handwriting.

My two older brothers teased me incessantly, saying, "You're insane. No way will you ever get a horse for Christmas! We don't even have a stable."

Right before opening the presents on Christmas Eve, my parents mysteriously disappeared. Then, the doorbell rang and the three of us ran to see who was there. When we opened the door, we saw standing in the snow a small Shetland pony with thick winter fur. Atop his back sat a little saddle. And next to him stood the three Magi. My parents had dressed up as Caspar and Belshazzar and my Uncle Winfried with his low voice provided Melchar. "We are on our way to Bethlehem," they said, trying to change their voices so we couldn't recognize them. "This little pony can't walk that far. So you have to take care of her for us. Can you do that?"

Overjoyed, I lunged at the pony and hugged her about the neck. "Yes! Oh, yes!" Her name was Ilse. Triumphantly, the three Magi walked little Ilse around to the new "garden" shed that had been built just a few weeks before. We had wondered why it had been fenced in. But, when we queried my parents, they said it was a pen for our big German Shepherd dog.

I stayed in the stable until late in the night, feeding Ilse oats and apples until I fell asleep in the hay and was carried to bed.

From that moment on, I was completely in love with Ilse and all the ponies that came after her. I spent most of my time in Ilse's paddock. I even rode to school on her. When I think back, I realize it was very generous of my mother to walk at my side and then bring Ilse back home every morning.

Each spring, my parents arranged for Ilse to visit another pony farm to get bred. My parents called it "going to get married." Naturally, I imagined Ilse all dressed up in a white dress. But, why did it happen every year?

The result, of course, was that there was a new foal almost every year. Until the arrival of Ilse, my childhood had been very lonely. My father was out of town most of the time. He was a famous Shakespearean scholar who was building a world-class library for the University of Munich. He loved me, but I only saw him on weekends.

My mother was even more distant. Although physically present, I can't ever remember being held by her. She was an accomplished Ph.D. who worked as a teacher and archeologist, but she was not learned in the ways of affection. In fact, at that time in Germany, many intellectuals believed that hugs spoiled a child. Too much affection and attention were definitely considered bad for children.

There was, however, a much beloved Aunt named Lore who truly cared for me. She often came to visit and showered us with hugs and attention. She and the pony were my salvation.

My happiest memories lay in the heart of the Bavarian countryside. Ilse and I would ride into the deep forests to commune with the dark evergreen trees and woodland creatures.

In my sixth year, a Frenchman visited our house, an acquaintance of my parents. He was about thirty some years or so and extremely handsome and charming with deep set eyes and dark hair. I fell in love. I remember clearly that I was allowed to say "Good Night" to him one evening and that I was completely taken by his beauty and presence to the point that I could not talk and just looked at him. I was very shy as a child, but in his presence even more so. But, I felt a tremendous feeling in my heart and stomach and even though nobody had ever told me anything about love, or being in love, or anything connected with it, I felt for the first time the overwhelming magic of the mystery of love!

As I was convinced that I would marry him, after he had left I asked my mother if she could help me write a letter to him, to at least let him know about his and my future together. So I wrote: "I will marry you. But, before that I have to learn French and then I can come to France and marry you."

I started my French lessons the next day with my wonderful and warmhearted grandmother and for one whole year we would meet every evening and she would teach me the basics of the French language. Every day I would wait for a letter from my 'Beloved'. I would dream about him and eagerly await the postman. My heart sank every morning when there was no letter. No letter ever came! It was my first experience of a broken heart and yet it probably was a blessing in disguise. I had learned some French and I had felt love. And, I didn't have to be married to a much older Frenchman after all.

The year of being six continued to be eventful. That fall, a woman came to our village school and played the flute for us children. I came home and said very firmly to my parents, "I will be a flutist." I knew that this was what I wanted and I left no room for any doubts. Guess what my parents did? They went out and bought me a violin! My father was quite accomplished on this beautiful instrument. But, after hearing me screech on the strings of a miniature violin for a few months, he gave in. I got a recorder and then bigger recorders and finally at age twelve the 'real thing,' my first 'flute traversiere,' and my love affair with the sound of the flute has never ceased.

When I was eleven or so, it was time to get a bigger pony. My feet touched the ground on tiny Ilse. My parents heard about a shipment of horses coming in to Bonn from Iceland. My mother and I went to select a hardy Icelandic pony for our home. I'll never forget the scene as about sixty ponies milled about in a large corral. They were drooping from their long journey.

I was immediately drawn to a very skinny and sickly-looking black horse. He stood by himself in the corner. I ran up and blew gently into his nose. This is a nice way to introduce yourself to a horse. You breathe into his nose, and he breathes your scent back. It's how they greet each other. An agent came up to my mother and me. "This is Svadi. I'm sorry, but he's already reserved for a lady in Switzerland. Maybe it's just as well, since he's quite sick from the trip." I was so disappointed, my heart dropped to my stomach as Svadi blew gently into my face. A much more beautiful horse was offered, a white female. But, I was in love with Svadi and very disappointed.

We went home to await the arrival of our new horse. Then, came an unexpected phone call, "The lady in Switzerland has changed her mind. Do you still want Svadi?"

I screamed with joy! A week later Svadi arrived, and our twenty-five year loving friendship and bond began, even though I believe it already was there when we first met. I always felt I had known Svadi from somewhere. He was my closest friend; my guardian angel, my advisor, my hero, my companion and we became inseparable. I rode him every afternoon and sometimes in the evening by moonlight.

Ilse was by now a grandmother and busy with her brood. One year Isa, one of Ilse's daughters, had a foal, but because Isa was still very young and inexperienced she kicked the new foal away and did not let her drink. We were all very concerned, as it was obvious that we would have to find an alternative to bring up the foal. Any efforts to get Isa to accept her foal failed. Then, a miracle of nature happened. Ilse, who at the time did not have a foal, suddenly stepped in and nursed the little newcomer. Just because she wanted to help with the nurturing she somehow produced milk. It was a manifestation of the power of love that can actually create physical changes.

Svadi and I learned to race and jump fences at horse shows. He was extremely fast and very competitive. He almost always won the race even against larger horses. They hated him at the shows and began to call him "the little Black Devil." Svadi had so much heart that he would throw himself over fences that were almost above his head. He was featured in the local newspaper when he won an important race. They liked his competitive spirit.

Whenever I had troubles with my brothers, or at school, I would talk to Svadi. I felt closer to him than to anyone. I played my recorder and flute for him, and he would close his eyes and sleep. Those concerts for my ponies turned out to be the best training for future cruise audiences!

Svadi saw me through my entire childhood and teenage years. When I left Bavaria to study in Munich, I would come home every weekend to see him. Later, when I went to live in Brazil, I missed him terribly and looked forward to being reunited with him on every trip home.

Svadi also became a local celebrity. Many young girls from the village would come to feed and ride him after I left home. He was famous in Endorf. Some of them even sent him letters and paintings of other horses so he wouldn't be lonely. My mother pinned them up on the walls of his stable.

My parents gradually sold all the other ponies, but we kept Svadi to the end. He finally got a bad cold and we had to put him out of his suffering at an amazing thirty-five years of age. I was not there when he died (I had moved to America), but I wrote him a long letter of thanks in my journal. I see him in my dreams to this day.

I believe animals can be our teachers and companions. If we really listen and are open-minded and openhearted, we can learn so much about the mysteries and rhythms of life through animals.

On all my concert tours, the most nourishing and regenerating experience for me is to go into nature and play for animals. They react very directly to sound and music. They, like us, are part of the song of life. The more we ignite our own love for all life, the more it touches others. Most animals are very responsive to unconditional love.

In my childhood, a camel in Bavaria responded to music I played on my flute. A small local circus used to camp near my home. When I visited the animals in their pens, I always took out my flute and played a small tune in celebration of them. I tried to express their particular melody, or inner song. To my delight, that camel used to sway and dance to my music. The sound and his dance communicated the essence of the interconnectedness—the music and the rhythm of life that lives in all life forms. Regardless of spiritual path, physical or animal bodies, or beliefs, this inner music touches and connects us soul to soul.

We all have music in our innermost selves. It can be our deepest connection to what we might call "all there is," God, the source. Our inner music reveals our true, divine nature. Sometimes, I feel moved to express the song of a dolphin, or a friend, or my deepest feelings. It is the source of many favorite compositions.

Many times, animals draw closer as I play. I have performed for donkeys, horses, kangaroos, birds, deer, camels, wombats, dogs, cats, dolphins, whales, penguins, crocodiles and many more. One time, I played my flute for a cobra in a basket on the streets of India. He or she immediately came out of the basket, reaching his or her full height of five feet. But, as the cobra leaned in for a kiss, I politely declined. I told him or her that I was flattered but that was enough. Animals' reactions to us differ, but like people they have favorites. I would want to be sure where I stood with a Cobra before embracing one.

Many birds call back with their songs—especially when I play the Norwegian flute as it has an unusual, trilling voice. On the North Cape of Norway I played the Tibetan flute for a reindeer. He started to breathe very oddly, sort of panting. Maybe he thought I was a sexy female reindeer!

One Easter Sunday morning, I found myself on a ship going from Dubai through the Suez Canal to Egypt. I was supposed to play *Amazing Grace* on my bass flute as part of the Easter Mass. It was held outside and the wind was blowing hard. There is no way that one can play the flute in the wind because the movement of the air simply takes the sound away. Six hundred people were looking at me in great expectation, as I walked up to the microphone and put the bass flute to my lips. I blew the first note: Nothing! I tried again: no sound— absolutely no notes came out because the wind snatched the sound before they could! I started to sweat! And then, suddenly I saw the dolphins! They had come out and were jumping and frolicking around the ship! I felt their joy and their energy and even though the wind was still blowing I picked up my gold flute and gave it one more shot. Now the sound came out and I managed to play through a whole verse of *Amazing Grace*. When I was done, the priest who was then supposed to read some Bible quote, mentioned: "I think the dolphins were sent by God to help Bettine this morning!" And yes, maybe they were sent, or maybe they heard my plight, and because we are all interconnected they showed up, and as they communicate through sound they joined us in a celebration of the real amazing grace that it is to be alive and to feel the love that connects us. Someone in the audience later told me that they counted twelve dolphins swimming beside the ship, but that might have been the interpretation of a Biblical scholar who liked the number twelve because of the twelve Apostles. I felt the miracle was their presence and not their number.

Pets are often masters at unconditional love. They hold no judgments regarding race, right and wrong, or status. They respond to feelings without opinion. By observing and living with them, we can absorb an important lesson: to simply be... to feel life without thinking. There is no need to define and analyze; just be present in the moment.

Take a moment to watch a dog. Ask yourself: Is he worried about his schedule next week; his paycheck; or is he maybe just listening to his grumbling stomach; getting excited about a cat stalking past him; or chasing another dog?

Most creatures that do not think so much have a very strong life force. This is due to always living in the now, the present moment. When you listen to music, you are also in the moment. The secret is to be present right here, now!

On the ship *Crystal Harmony* I played *Love Song to a Planet*, a song that came to me in the rain forest near the Amazon River. It was given to me as an inner melody that I wrote down, and has since become one of my most popular pieces. A recording of jungle parrots and toucans accompanies me as I play against a backdrop of exotic slides from the huge canopy of Brazilian trees.

Naturally, I practiced in my cabin every day. Cabin walls are sometimes pretty thin. The fitness instructor for the ship was bunking next door, and asked about the strange sounds from my cabin. Awakened from a deep musical reverie, I said, "Well, I'm just practicing with the birds for my concert."

The next thing I knew, a rumor was circulating on board that I had upward of thirty birds from the Amazon in my cabin! Passengers would come up to me and ask: "When can we see your birds?" I would tell them: "Definitely not before the show, because they freak out, they get too nervous! Maybe you can see them after my first show!"

On the last day of the cruise, I received a phone call from the front desk. "You have to come immediately to show your birth certificate," they informed me. "I don't travel with my birth certificate," I replied in puzzlement. "I only have my passport, but I'm sure I was born, that's pretty obvious." Then, I ran to the reception desk. An official in a uniform waited for me there and clarified the matter; "I don't want your *birth* certificate. I need your *bird* certificate—the paperwork that allows you to travel with all those birds in your cabin! Come with me."

We stepped into a small room where five other officials were sitting around a table. They had a number of forms prepared for me. "Where is your bird license?" one of them asked. "The provisions manager told us you have thirty birds in your cabin."

I struggled to explain even though there was a slight language barrier. "These birds exist, but they are invisible. They are in my music. They are on a tape." It took some fast-talking and a review of my cabin to resolve the dilemma. But, they enjoyed it when I played them the rain forest song with the tape of the birds. And the story has given many friends and me healing doses of laughter. Humor, love, and music can connect us all, and with those elements we can all play a great symphony in harmony—humans, animals, plants and all life forms together.

# Chapter Two

# A Life-Changing Car Accident

I grew up with Svadi in the Bavarian countryside. Our home was in a small town called Endorf. It was close to Munich, but surrounded by many lakes and forests. My parents followed traditional German values in raising us, but in matters of religion and spirituality, we were outcast Protestants in a Catholic community. I remember the fear instilled in us at school. Our religion teachers were always warning us about the Devil—that he was inside us, and we must always resist him. My brothers and I even were told to burn the Devil puppet in our toy "Punch and Judy" show! And, we did, just out of that fear. I remember my brother Christian once sitting in a depressed state in front of our house at the age of seven or eight and saying: "Religion spoils my whole life!" But, there were some advantages to Religion in my childhood. The Lutheran Pastor was one of the few people in the village who had TV in his house. We never had TV in our own house when we were growing up. So, my brothers and I often went to the Lutheran Pastor's house to watch TV. Sometimes, we said we were going over there to study the Catechism, but we hated the Catechism and fortunately the Pastor liked us coming over to watch TV.

My father was a scholar and a free thinker. Despite his liberal advice however, our house was not too joyful. We always had to be quiet so he could work. This meant we were often sent to the Garden House to stay out of his way. I grew up very alone except for my close relationship with Svadi. My only other loves were nature and music, with the additional hugs of my one affectionate aunt.

In looking back, it was no surprise that I took such an intense interest in boys when I became twelve. Apart from the fact that my two older brothers were well into girls by that time, I was looking for tenderness, attention, and love. My once lonely life became a whirl of parties and boyfriends.

When I was sixteen, I met a young man from Sweden who gave me that tenderness for which I was looking. It was love at first sight as soon as I met Joern at a party. We each felt a deep connection. He was ten years older than I was which probably scared my parents. But, he was very sensitive and put no pressures on me to grow up too fast. This tender first love displaced even Svadi. Joern talked of spending our lives together. We enjoyed every moment of our romance—picnics, drives in the country, talking and long dinner dates. Then fate intervened. One evening, as Joern was driving me home from a party, a front tire suddenly exploded. The car veered out of control and pitched headlong into a tree.

I remembered little of the accident. All I could see in my mind's eye was the car crumpling against the tree, as I looked down on it from way up above. I turned away and was caught up with my boyfriend in another dimension. Tremendous waves of love and acceptance swept over Joern and me. I felt so light. We were together, forever. But, then I noticed a slight separation—an invisible barrier like a glass wall had come between us. I couldn't quite reach him anymore. I was alone, hanging in a timeless, light-filled space. All was well, but I couldn't accompany Joern, even though I loved him. He was destined for another journey. Music, beautiful music, surrounded me. All then turned to a brilliant white light.

Physically, my life was in danger. I had slipped into a coma that lasted the whole night. When I woke up in the hospital, I immediately tried to ask the nurses about Joern. They didn't tell me my boyfriend had died, but I knew it intuitively. When I asked, they turned their faces away and said he was in intensive care. My mother and father were so relieved that I was going to be all right. On my third day in the hospital my mother told me as gently as she could that Joern had died. Emotionally, I slipped under the waves of grief. I had lost my first great love. I didn't know if I could go on living.

A long period of pain followed for my broken heart along with my body. I spent many weeks flat on my back and full of despair. My face was in stitches from the shattered windshield. I had terrible concussion that caused headaches and nausea. But, whenever I would feel truly hopeless, my mind would wander back to that light and the haunting music that had enveloped me high above the accident accompanied by that feeling of unconditional, limitless love.

This timeless little bubble of experience buoyed me though the grief. I couldn't really think of ending my life despite my total despair. I knew I was loved. Someone, or something, had cared enough to lift me into that sea of light and ethereal sound. I longed to go back to that wonderful world. The near-death experience had transformed my view of life forever. I knew that this life was but a small part of something far greater. I knew that our essence lives forever, and that we are an endless melody.

For a while, I had many dreams with Joern. He would always say, "I'm not really back, I have to return in the morning."

"Where to?" I would ask. "Stay with me."

I always felt comforted, even though I woke up alone. The connection was still there. In fact, these tender dreams stayed with me for eight full years. Then they abruptly ended. The spirit of my beloved friend told me he had to move on. I never saw him again, but his gift of love lingered.

This car accident became a catalyst for my profound spiritual search. As I recuperated, I studied many religions and teachings: Buddhism, Christian mysticism, TM (which I embraced fanatically), and many other paths. I eventually found a teaching called Eckankar, which I liked because it encouraged people to chant in contemplation—to sing sacred words to themselves for upliftment. 'This is right up my alley,' I thought. Something about that incredible music left me believing in sound as a way to touch the face of God.

I tried singing an ancient name for God called "Hu." I simply hummed it over and over, out loud. Immediately, light and sound surrounded me; I was in the same place where I had been with my boyfriend. Then, I got scared of this feeling, and returned to TM, but the memory enlivened me.

During the following years, I matured and began my adult life growing ever busier and more ambitious. I was offered a position with the Munich Bach Orchestra, a great honor. I practiced all the time when I was not rushing to rehearsals. I pressed myself to fulfill my potential. But, somewhere in this rush, I began to lose my teenage spirituality. The Bach Orchestra was planning a great concert tour to the USA. I was excited about it and threw myself into packing and preparing to go on the road. My attitude was one of pushing, rather than openness, or receptivity to life. I was becoming a little bit brittle, somewhat hard. The changes were subtle, but there was a shift in my purpose. I was no longer living to express love and music, but to get things done. I was doing instead of being. In all this rush, I needed to look for a way to relax, but instead of paying attention to life and slowing down, I went home and raced my horses. I still remembered my near-death experience, but I felt compelled to keep it to myself. In those days in the late "Sixties" in Bavaria, hardly anybody would have understood such things. 'Should I... could I... reorganize my life to live in a more spiritual way? What would that look like to my peers in the Orchestra? Who had time to think anyway?'

I took Cygnet, our very spirited Connemara pony, out for a ride. Restless, I urged him on faster and faster. To get my mind into the moment required thrills and physical challenges. All of a sudden, a dog ran out of the bushes. He savagely bit at Cygnet's legs scaring him so he reared up shrieking in fear. Unprepared, I fell backward from the saddle directly onto a rock. Immediately, I knew something was drastically wrong. I couldn't move. The pain was so strong that all I could do was scream.

Fortunately, some neighbors heard me and called for help before running to my side. As I lay in the hospital, I was informed I had broken my back. Several vertebrae were injured and I would be in a cast for at least two months. At first, it was not certain that I would ever walk again. I was frantic about missing the great tour of the Orchestra. I couldn't stand the disappointment. But, gradually I began to wonder why this had happened just now. I have always tried to make the best of every situation—but this was a challenge. As the days trickled by, I reassessed. Perhaps how one lives and does things is as important as what we do. Was I out of tune with my life's song? Here was a chance to truly reflect on my purpose. Maybe I wasn't exactly listening to my highest inner leanings. Possibly accomplishment wasn't the only goal. Perhaps my attitude and thoughts were as important as what I achieved. I decided to express in my music the mystical connection that I had experienced in my car accident. This meant paying attention and resonating with the moment. I needed to let life's song come through me.

Slowly, I began to move again. Physical therapy began with flexing movements and slow stretching in a large pool of water. Gradually, I began to walk through the pool letting the water support my weight. I began to learn how to live that way, too, letting life support me and carry me forward. I didn't need to push, but only swim with the current. I learned that gratitude carried me through and made this swimming easier, like wearing a life belt.

During this time, my nighttime dreams kept leading me forward. I would return to that ocean of love, light and sound that had encompassed me after my first accident. I began to sing "Hu" again, and in my dreams I encountered some of the spiritual Masters of Eckankar called Eck Masters. The message seemed to be to go within. During the day, my bedside window looked out at the castle of King Ludwig at Herreninsel on Lake Chiemsee. The beauty of a new sunrise every morning seemed to pull me inside. After a night of intense dreaming I would daydream gazing at the magnificent castle, King Ludwig's replica of Versailles. It was a symbol of what I could create with my life—a shining fortress of calm and beauty for my own and others' upliftment.

This accident, like the first, was a definite gift. I had to let go of my ambitions for fame, acknowledgment, and ego-gratification. Instead, I began to play for love, and love alone. The only flute I could raise to my lips while in the cast was my piccolo. Even then my arms quickly grew too heavy. So I decided to concentrate on my breathing— important for any wind instrument. If I couldn't play long for love, I could breathe for love. Breathing is the most important, simple, and basic spiritual exercise one can do each day. Most people never think of breathing as a spiritual activity, but it can be!

First, I began with a simple exercise—breathing in circles. This means you connect the in-breath with the out-breath, imagining a golden, connected circle. It makes your music smoother and more relaxed. Then, I started to experiment with yogi breathing. Soon, I came to view taking a simple breath as the most transforming practice in my life. Breathing is the essence of life—if the breath leaves the body, the life-force leaves with it. The breath and the life force, or "Prana," are closely connected. The more breath you bring in, the more life force you have. Most of the time we tend to ignore our breath, inhaling shallowly from the top of our lungs.

Place your hand on your abdomen. Take a deep breath, letting it push out your stomach. Feel it with your hand. Concentrate on breathing in life, and breathing out tension. Relax and inhale. Release and exhale.

I believe this simple exercise can bring more spiritual awareness into each cell of your being. If you spend a few minutes at it each day, you'll be amazed at the insights that come, the worries that are released, and how much more centered and calm you feel. I personally try to do twenty connected breathing cycles a day. I breathe in and out without stopping and without being distracted. It's important to breathe very deeply. If you are in a stress situation, you're only a breath away from being relaxed, light-hearted, and joyful again. It's so easy.

As I was studying the spiritual side of breathing, some friends told me that our breathing patterns are established from the very time of our birth. When we were born, the doctors might have cut the cord very early in the process, perhaps before we were ready. For many of us, it might have felt like suffocating. Panic or stress re-activates this earliest feeling, and we shut down our breathing. But, taking in air very deeply and slowly helps return us to a safe place, to warmth and love.

Flute playing energizes and heals me, and a lot of that is related to all the breath I expend. Actually, many things happen at once. The sound in itself is healing. Anytime you produce sound—sing, laugh, or play an instrument—you are connecting all of your cells with that sound. It's like lining up metal filings with a magnet. Thoughts stop. The music fills you and aligns you with a higher force, the life force.

We don't know it, but quite often our thoughts are about ourselves and most of these self-thoughts are negative. One key to inner peace and freedom is to be able to release thought altogether, or at least choose what we want to think about. We each live in a stream of thoughts. When they are serene and loving toward ourself and others, they can transform our world. This is not something we're taught to do—to choose our thoughts. But, uplifting music helps. Instead of forcing us to think the right thoughts, it can gradually release tension so we naturally feel good about ourselves.

Here's another simple exercise to try. Look in the mirror right now and say to yourself, "I love you and we're going to have a great day!" This is not egotism, but loving yourself as soul. You are a spiritual being with an emotional, mental, and physical body and they only work when infused with love. It seems to work. It reinforces a positive self-image, a picture of that shining castle that we truly are. We don't often give ourselves unconditional love.

Our bodies reflect whatever we believe and think, which is our life's music or song. This is because life is a hologram. Science is finally discovering the principle of the hologram. Whatever thought you think is creative of a whole. What we put out as a thought will be manifested as a condition or state in our perception sooner or later.

What else did I discover while recovering from my broken back? Certainly that we have an inner, imaginary life that can help us live more happily and easily every day. All it takes is a bit of commitment to quiet time each day. When we use our imagination to travel within to another dimension, there is skill involved, but there is also a reality to our inner world. At first we may think it is just our imagination, but soon a higher reality takes over. Our contemplations will take on lives of their own.

Most of my compositions, good ideas, inspirations, and encouragement come from this simple daily time spent looking within. I suggest to you to try just ten minutes of it right now—and every day from here on. Set a regular time. You're worth it.

# Chapter Three

# *Adventures in Brazil*

In my twenties, I made a decision to follow my childhood dream of exploring the whole world. At the time, I was a flautist with the prestigious Salzburg Mozarteum Orchestra in Austria. I was sitting in rehearsals one day reading a newspaper when I saw an ad: "Solo Flutist Wanted in Brazil." Somehow it ignited my imagination. I knew I had to get out and explore life beyond Salzburg and conventional Europe. Perhaps this was to be the next step in my life's journey.

That evening, after taking a deep breath, I called the number listed in the paper. I reached a representative for a new Brazilian orchestra. He said they would soon be in Europe to audition players. I agreed to try out for them in Munich. The orchestra was to be an international group made up of Brazilians, Americans and Europeans. The city in which they would play was called Belo Horizonte, which means "Beautiful Horizon." I did not speak any Portuguese, but I felt that the name Belo Horizonte sounded so musical and beautiful and I knew intuitively that I would go there.

I went into the audition with confidence and the intention to move to Brazil. I got the job, and within a few months I had resigned from my safe and reputable position in the Salzburg orchestra; packed many of my belongings and my nine different flutes into boxes; taken about three lessons in Portuguese from a retired Brazilian priest who had been deported from Brazil because of his socialist leanings in his work for the poor; and I had headed towards Belo Horizonte.

One of the very first things I discovered on my arrival was that Brazil with its hot climate moves according to the "amanha" or "manhana" rhythm of life. There's always time to do something "amanha," or "tomorrow" instead of today. But, what a perfect opportunity to learn patience, and especially for someone coming from Germany where one can set one's watch by the punctuality of the trains. The orchestra did not have a very clear mission, or if it had one it did not really manifest. But, I was busy taking in the sights and sounds of the exotic surroundings of Belo Horizonte—the rain forest, the wonderful smells and the warmhearted people. One of the founders of the orchestra was kind enough to take me into her house for a while until I sought out a place of my own. She lived with her family of four, half an hour outside of town and very close to the jungle. I became fascinated by the breathtaking beauty of the raw wilderness of the animal and plant world and by the intoxicating smells that emanated from this nearby forest.

The orchestra was in a chaotic state. But, I decided not to worry about that too much. One of the things in our lives we can control is our thoughts and attitudes. I found that taken with humor all the disorganization and tomorrow-philosophy was actually a great break from the rigidity of Germany and Austria. My real job was simply to be a pioneer in my own life. Language, of course, was a barrier. At first, I couldn't understand a word of Portuguese. But, after a few weeks of visiting the market, the local shops, and sightseeing, my musical ear began to work on my behalf. I could understand the gist of things if I thought of the sounds as music. 'If I listen closely with an open heart,' I told myself, 'I will begin to sing and play this strange Portuguese music.' I also realized that the Latin I had learned in school was not for nothing as all the words in Portuguese have a Latin root.

Here was my first opportunity to live far from my hometown in Bavaria, out of the reach of my family. "Why not make the most of this adventure?" I said to myself. I had to reassure my father many times in those first uncertain weeks, telling him and myself not to worry about all the unknown areas of my new life.

My boxes and flutes were shipped to the little mountain town in the province of Minas Gerais. I found a little cottage on the edge of the rain forest, truly on the brink of civilization. I called it my little dream house. Exotic smells wafted in from the open windows, not to mention strange snakes and spiders that at times visited me from the jungle. The sounds at night were incredible. I felt like Rima from *Green Mansions*. Often I would take in the beauty of the jungle as I drove back to my dream house from an evening concert. The fragrances of the flowers were seductive as I anticipated my evening reunion with a new family member who had adopted me.

One morning, I'd opened the door to find a little gray dog wagging his tail and looking lovingly into my eyes. I told him over and over to go home, but, after a day or two, I knew he wanted to stay with me. I went out and got some food for him and decided to give him the name of a French man I admired named Cyril.

My adopted dog Cyril and I enjoyed long walks during which I confided in him about my many difficulties with my uncertain life in Brazil. He was such a good listener and we quickly became best friends. Every day, I looked forward to coming home to his loving care.

A few weeks later, my life became exceptionally busy. The Orchestra was to perform a major concert and with such an international mix of musicians it was quite a task to get it into shape. I experienced a week from hell. Intense rehearsals filled my days and to crown it, at the same time, the government told me I would have to file many new documents to stay in the country. There was also the frustration of my teaching position, which seemed to reach a crisis at that time. My contract was not only to play solo flute in the orchestra, but also to be a professor of flute at the Conservatory. I was assigned about five Brazilian students, but in the first weeks I did not immediately know about the country's time concept. So when we arranged for a 2:00 p.m. lesson, the student usually showed up at 3:30 p.m. thinking that this was perfectly all right. When I eventually caught on, and thus arrived later myself after these tedious rehearsals, I found some sympathetic students had started to show up on time! In short, most days we missed each other! Between the rehearsals, the inefficient bureaucracy, and my efforts to teach these flute lessons, I hardly had time to feed Cyril let alone talk to him, before dashing off first thing in the morning and not returning until late at night. I knew it was neglectful to forgo talking to him, but life seemed like a non-stop emergency. Finally, the time-consuming concert came. Once it was over, I was free for a few days, and as I returned home in the muggy steaming heat of a Brazilian evening, I looked forward to sharing those days with Cyril.

Cyril always waited for me at the gate, but that night he wasn't there. I walked around the house calling his name. I thought maybe he was hiding in the garden? There was no answer.

My heart stopped. 'Where is he?' I asked myself. This little ball of fur had provided me with months of comfort. 'What if something has happened to him?'

I looked for him for over an hour in the dark meadow around the house and even ventured into the pitch-black jungle. I couldn't see a thing. Eventually, I gave up and went to bed.

The next morning, my search continued. I went into the hills and walked for hours calling, "Cyril! Cyril!" Deep within, I knew something was wrong. Sadly, I returned home, sat in a chair and wept. 'Is he gone forever?' I thought, my few days of vacation had been ruined by this probable reality.

Over the following weeks, I continued my search between teaching, rehearsals, government appointments, and concerts. I asked all my neighbors to keep an eye out for him. I felt so terribly guilty because before he disappeared I hadn't given my dog friend all the love and attention he deserved.

Finally, I gave up. Now, my goal was simply to discover what had happened. I asked God to show me. Weeks later, a neighboring rancher came by. He lived about an hour away and had heard that I was missing Cyril. He put his head down and told me a car killed the little dog not far from where he lived.

Devastated, I cried for several days. 'I was the reason he went away and got killed,' I thought. 'Cyril needed more love, and I was too busy.' My heart felt weak and broken.

But, one night I had a dream. Cyril was running toward me, his eyes sparkling with life. He threw himself into my arms and licked my face. Without words, he transmitted a message to my heart. 'Do not worry or grieve. I am happy. I loved my time with you. It wasn't your fault I left. I just wanted to move on to another adventure.' Then, we spent some more time together in the dream, enjoying this unconditional love. When I woke up, my grief had lifted.

I will never forget Cyril. He taught me two very important lessons. First and foremost, always take very good care of those who come into your life as companions, guardians, and friends. Being busy shouldn't get in the way of love. I felt this interconnectedness with Cyril as I had with my horses in my childhood. I think the lesson I

learned was: 'Take good care of other souls, for they are a part of you.'
Secondly, I felt I learned not to let guilt cloud my life but to let love
shine forth instead. Much later when my mother died, I would
desperately need this second message.

After losing Cyril, I took some local sightseeing trips. There was
only one problem. Every time I was gone for more than a day or two,
a thief invaded my home. I didn't have much, but he would relieve me
of a small tape-player, some cassettes, and whatever else I had lying
around.

Meanwhile, the orchestra would rehearse for weeks, only to have
its concert schedule collapse. Arrangements for the concert hall or the
soloist would fall through. When this happened, instead of worrying, I
decided to take advantage of these opportunities to visit Argentina,
Peru, Ecuador, Bolivia, and Uruguay. These journeys of several days
turned out to be great adventures. Whenever I arrived in some town, I
would try to hook up with local musicians or authorities and offer to
do a workshop or musical performance. Often they would set something
up for me.

I became especially fond of Peru with its ancient, mystical ruins.
On one trip, I set out to climb up to an ancient city in the hills above
Cusco. Soon I realized I was to be accompanied by another adventurer,
a Peruvian man. We fell in step, and I discovered that he was an
archeologist of about my age. After some desultory conversation, we
found we were both born in the same year, on the same day, and even
at the exact same hour, but in opposite corners of the earth. I know he
wasn't making it up, because he volunteered his birthday and date
first. The archeologist spoke only broken English, but soon I had my
own personal tour of the ruins and some caves, which I would never
have discovered otherwise.

That afternoon, we entered a cave and paused to perch on a rock
for a moment's rest. Suddenly, the whole space filled with white light!
A picture of my companion in ancient Inca dress flashed before me. I
also saw myself in an Inca outfit. Did we have a past-life connection,
or had he lived in this earlier time? Who knows? But, the experience
was very vivid and I have never forgotten it.

During this adventure, I learned a very valuable skill: how to
synchronize myself to the music of strange cultures and places. I
became very alert to the rhythms and vibrations of each new location.
Next on my agenda was Machu Pichu. The whole city nestled into the

mountain in such a harmonious way. It took my breath away when I first glimpsed it. 'How could the Spaniards and Portuguese have destroyed this?' I wondered. I definitely felt I'd been there before—a kind of deja vu experience.

I returned home for a concert or two, finding the usual mess from my mysterious burglar. But, the orchestra was still having problems, so in a matter of weeks I went traveling again, this time flying to La Paz, Bolivia and boarding a bus there purportedly bound for famed Titicaca lake. At the bus station, they told me the trip would take four hours. After six hours went by, I began to ask my fellow passengers what was going on. "Este onibus va para Titicaca?" I asked in my broken Spanish. Everybody in the bus shook his or her head. "No, no, no, este onibus va para Ururu!" So, it turned out that I was on the wrong bus and on my way to some place called Ururu of which I had never heard. I decided to just go with it. There really was not anything else to do. We finally arrived in Ururu at the time of a huge carnival attended by thousands of revelers. I stayed for two days, meeting many wonderful people and enjoying their local crafts, customs, foods and the fascinating sounds of the Bolivian panpipes.

High in the mountains of Bolivia, above La Paz at perhaps 15,000 feet, I encountered a woman in a small cabin. I was hiking in this dramatic countryside. I was used to the Alps, but this was much higher causing me to be out of breath. As I walked past her doorway, she smiled and gestured to me. I went into her cabin and she offered me an odd-smelling tea. Using hand signs, she indicated that it would help me cope with the altitude. We spent a few very precious hours together. I played the flute for her (I always carry one with me), and then departed. No words were necessary. It's hard to describe the connection we had. There was no effort on either side. It just was.

On my return to Belo Horizonte, I found my dream house in total chaos again. The thief had thrown everything on the floor, but only taken my newest tape player, just like before. I had marvelous books in Spanish, German, English, and Portuguese, but these he never touched. I was almost offended.

I decided to get a new dog for protection. I don't know if it was a joke, but the local people offered me a tiny specimen weighing no more than five pounds, whom I named Lara. She had the most beautiful eyes, and reminded me of Lara in *Doctor Zhivago*. She was a puppy of only five months and in the first week at my house she fell into a bucket of red paint. I managed to fish her out in time and tried really hard to get the red color out of her coat but without success. Lara stayed pink her whole life.

The thief got bolder and his next visit came while I was at home. Fortunately, Lara barked. With my heart in my throat, I saw the man lifting the push-up window that I'd opened to let in the breeze. It was eerie. My mind raced, trying to figure out what to do next. Suddenly, I heard beautiful music fill my ears and drift through the whole house. It was that sound current that had always brought so much peace and love into my life over the last twenty years and that I had heard for the first time in my accident when I was outside of my body. Then, there was a big crash. The window slammed down on the thief's hand! He screamed and fled. It must have hurt a lot, although I didn't find any dismembered fingers when I rushed to the sill. I thanked this protecting force—my inner guidance that had come to me in this inner music.

The next morning, I went to the police to report the thief. Five burglaries seemed enough and I guess I finally got the message—'It's time to do something about this.' The policeman to whom I spoke told me he had to visit the scene of the crime, so we walked back to my little house. But, once inside, he started to press himself against me! I had to be pretty firm. To live as a woman alone by the jungle was not the best idea. I decided to move into a different village, where there were more people and greater protection. Friends told me about a beautiful three-story house with several fireplaces that was available for a very low rent. There was only one drawback: there was no water in the house! But, through this I learned how to draw water with a bucket from the nearby well. One sure becomes economical in one's water usage if one knows how much "schlepping" is involved!

The orchestra definitely had its star moments! We played music by the great composers such as Beethoven, Mozart, Brahms, Mahler, Strauss and also some Brazilian composers like Villa-Lobos. I also started a small Brazilian combo consisting of two celli, percussion, guitar and flute and we played many concerts featuring fiery Brazilian music. I felt more and more at home in Brazil as her music spoke to me.

Later the same year it rained for three months straight, and the grass in my little garden grew about six feet tall. I had wonderful friends who often invited me to their huge fazenda (ranch), and when the rancher saw the grass in my garden, he sent me a horse and a saddle.

The horse was supposed to graze down the grass. I was overjoyed about this small light brown and sweet mare and named her Swana. And so Swana and Lara became my best companions.

Swana was a true Brazilian—she was very slow. In fact, she never moved much at all. She just stood in her paddock. But, shortly after acquiring her, a countrywide political revolution took place. I didn't know what it all meant, except that there was no imported food and no gas. Soon, my little Fiat car ran out of gas. There was no way I could get into town for rehearsals unless I went on horseback. The way Swana moved it would have taken me six to seven hours. I decided to just stay home and enjoy this unexpected vacation.

One morning, I heard a loud noise at the gate to my garden. I ran out and saw a beautiful horse rattling and pushing against the iron door. Swana was running around on the inside of the garden, acting very excitedly. I had an intuition about what this could mean, but wasn't quite sure. I opened the gate and the horse, which obviously was a stallion, galloped in and ran towards Swana, and they started this love play eventually coupling. I had seen this once before in my younger years, but never in that passion and intensity. They were making sounds of pleasure and they looked really beautiful together, as the stallion was of the same color as Swana, just bigger and more muscular. After they were done, they grazed together and just hung out. They seemed really in love. He mounted her three more times in the next two days and then, when I opened the gate again, he just left. Horses can be fickle too! He had done what he came to do, and it was time for him to go on to other things and other mares. Several months later it was obvious that Swana was pregnant and after eleven months she had a beautiful light brown foal. I had received another unexpected gift.

As the political unrest continued, the atmosphere grew worse. We, the European and American musicians of the orchestra, often had to stand in lines for four to five hours to process administrative forms in order to stay in the country. Many times the officials would just shut the window and say, "Come back tomorrow." Humor was the key to surviving such nonsense. Once, I was waiting at an office along with other musicians. The guy trying to help us didn't understand a word we said in any language. Whether in frustration or helplessness, I just burst out laughing, and then he started to laugh. Eventually, the whole office joined in except for one of my frustrated American friends who kept yelling obscenities. But, the humor got our papers stamped and us on our way home. This lighthearted approach to life has often helped me out.

Finally, it became clear that the orchestra was folding. I sold my car and began to pack and prepare for my departure to Europe. On my last day in Brazil, I was to deliver my car to its new owner, but I unknowingly parked it in the wrong place. The authorities towed it to some mysterious location. I knew from hard-won experience that it could take weeks or months to get a car out of the impound lot. I was due to leave Brazil on a flight in a matter of hours! I finally located the right office, and they told me that the process for getting my car back might take a month and a half. I didn't know whether to laugh or cry, but I had my flute with me and instead of arguing I just gave it a shot and started playing for the police officials. Pretty soon they began to clap and move to the music and shouted: "Mais um!" which means: "One more!" After four songs, the official behind the desk released the car. I delivered it to the new owner and dashed to the airport. When the plane finally lifted off Brazilian ground I looked out the window, watching the jungle disappear underneath the clouds and I quietly cried. My tears were mixed emotions of joy and sadness, and a heartfelt gratitude for a wonderful experience.

I had learned so much in this beautiful and diverse country—mostly to relax more, to have patience, and to live in the flow of life. Brazil taught me to not impose my way of living on others, but to respect and appreciate their culture and way of life. I learned to enjoy the diversity and newness of a different country and it invoked my own inner strength and helped me to grow. "Sempre tem jeito" is a popular Brazilian saying. It means, "There's always a way." They say that a lot. And now, so do I. It sure helps to find creative solutions. Worrying never achieves anything. There is always light at the end of the tunnel.

# Chapter Four

# An Alien in China

I returned to Europe on vacation once or twice while I was working in Brazil. On one such winter vacation, I went to a seminar on spirituality and met there a tall, handsome and shy American named Harold Ware who expressed an interest in going skiing with me. I told him that I had arranged to go out to the slopes with three friends, but that he was more than welcome to join us. For whatever reasons, or as fate would have it, my other friends never showed up, so Harold and I went skiing alone. To make a short story even shorter, we fell in love on the slopes. We felt a strong soul connection and both knew that we would see each other again. We did.

A few months later, after leaving Brazil and moving to the US, I was a married "alien" as they charmingly call non-US citizens. I lived in California with Harold, but I was without an agent, a job, or friends. It was sobering and humbling to start my career all over again. The Munich Bach and the Salzburg Mozarteum were both prestigious orchestras, and Europe also offers a musician much support through its many smaller orchestras and individual concert venues. Europeans have a long-established love for the arts. In America, I simply wasn't famous enough, and no one had any idea how to build my career. It might have been possible to play in a very large orchestra and offer lessons to local flutists, but this path seemed to offer no hope of performing my own music, which is what I really wanted to do. I also love to communicate one-on-one with audiences. So, I started my new career by playing some evenings at a tiny café in downtown Menlo Park, California. At first, I would take home a whopping $7.00 in tips for a whole evening of playing. And even that I had to split with the pianist! But, at least these tiny concerts gave me an outlet for my music.

Life was hard for a time. It takes great patience to start locally and work one's way up into national bookings. But, finally I got a larger concert. This gave me a lift, but it's still hard to break into the concert world in America. I called several agencies that told me, "We only book big names." I felt like calling down their phone lines—"Bettine Luise Adeline Clemen Ware is a pretty big name!" It was hard, but I persevered.

Finally, at a San Francisco-area concert I met Richard Patterson who plays classical guitar. We hit it off immediately both musically and personally and began working together. At one of our concerts, we met a man from China. He was a professor and director of the music conservatory in Shanghai. He asked about my music and training. I told him that I had studied with James Galway, Nicolet, Peter Lukas Graf, and Julius Baker, and that I had a Master's degree from the Staatliche Musikhochschule in Munich. I informed him I had played as a soloist and a member of all these European Orchestras. He seemed very happy to meet me, but in the crush of people the conversation soon slipped from my mind.

Months later, to my surprise a large, official envelope arrived in the mail from the Chinese government. I opened it to find an unusual invitation: "We would be honored if you would come to Beijing and Shanghai to teach master flute classes in residence and also perform four concerts. Please reply immediately."

I checked my schedule and wrote that I could come in March of that year, which was 1985. Within a few weeks, I was transported to Shanghai via Japan Airlines. I carefully chose four flutes with different registers: my regular 'C' flute in gold, my alto flute, bass flute and piccolo, to use in my teaching and performances. After a day and a half of travel, I wearily arrived at Shanghai airport with only a few phrases of Chinese, spoken with a strong German accent. A young man named Zhang approached me and introduced himself as my interpreter for the Shanghai conservatory. He was carrying a huge photograph of me, which I found somewhat amusing. Obviously, he thought this would make it easier for me to recognize him as my escort, but in reality, looking at it from my point of view, it would not have been too difficult for him to recognize me among the thousands of Chinese people at the airport. Assuredly, I was the only blonde there and one of only a handful of Europeans! With him were two professors. One specialized in flute, the other in trombone. The four of us got into a small car and were immediately surrounded by thousands of bicycles. Some heads turned as they saw my face for not many Westerners were visiting China at that time. My new companions were greatly amused by my few phrases of what they called "Chinglish." We established an immediate rapport that would stand us in good stead over the next few weeks.

At the Conservatory, all three gentlemen escorted me to my room, which was in the house for foreign professors. We had been there just two minutes when Zhang rubbed his hands together briskly and said, "Now we will discuss your schedule." I was dead tired, but work and discipline are primary in China. My schedule was to be as follows: For the next nine days, I would teach each morning from 8:30 a.m. until Noon. After lunch, I would rehearse with the orchestra and the string quartet for a concert on April 5th. Additionally, on several afternoons I would also teach workshops on different aspects of flute playing such as breath control, orchestral phrasing, practice and preparation for a performance. It was a thorough and rigorous training. But, I was happy to acquiesce. Early the next morning, the work began. It was a joy to instruct the most talented students chosen from among a billion people!

During the next few days, I heard some fifteen flutists ranging in age from nine to thirty. All were students of Lin Keh-Ming, and their musicality reflected his great dedication as a teacher. Fortunately, he spoke English and was able to relay my comments. We became very good friends.

The first evening, the Conservatory offered a customary banquet for me. Professor Li Mingqianj, a world-famous pianist and the Deputy Director of the Conservatory officially welcomed me. The fifteen-course meal lasted for four hours as we talked and exchanged stories about music. The people exhibited overwhelming hospitality and hunger for knowledge of European music and culture. They absorbed every possible bit of information and energy that I was able to exude.

The next afternoon, all the wind-instrument players came to a workshop on breath control. We discussed, and I demonstrated, how a well-supported sound gains in richness and expression. They asked me how to cope with shaking knees, trembling lips and short, uncontrolled breath when you're nervous at a performance. That led naturally into how to prepare for a concert. The hours passed so quickly.

My rehearsals with the string quartet and the chamber orchestra increased as our concert neared. I was impressed with their technical virtuosity. Conductor Whang always had a wonderful smile on his face as he led us through the pieces, which certainly helped everybody's playing. I had probably played under fifteen to twenty different conductors at this point, but I don't remember any of them smiling!

One morning I was introduced to Tan Mi-zi, a composer and the first-chair symphony flutist. He was filled with delight and enthusiasm for both life and music. He brought his piece for solo flute called *Flute and Drums under the Setting Sun*, which I was to perform during my concert. We spent the morning working on the piece, which starts with a percussion effect that leads into haunting, beautiful Chinese melodies. I later included it on an album I recorded named *Dancing in Sound*.

My last workshop in Shanghai was on improvisation. I started to improvise in different styles rather late in my flute career, but I find it helps my performances in the classical field and is excellent for ear training. I asked the class if they had ever improvised. They all shook their heads expressing, 'No… Never.' We started with a method I have used in recent years. It is like exchanging a question and an answer with flutes. At first, it is helpful to select just one or two keys or to choose the pentatonic scale. The main hurdle is the fear of playing wrong notes. So instead of wrong notes, I told the class there are just good or not-so-good choices. As we began, I went around in a circle, asking each flutist a question with my flute. I was amazed by their immediate and stimulating answers. It was as if they had been doing this for a long time. At the end of the workshop, everyone had overcome the fear of improvising, because they had already succeeded a few times. We had much fun in communicating in this way. It ended my stay on a high note!

The last day in Shanghai came too soon. I enjoyed my work there so much. Every moment had been lived to the fullest. That morning, we had a dress rehearsal. It was bitterly cold in the hall, and I could barely see through the cloud of my breath nor move my freezing fingers. The heating systems were turned off on March 1st regardless of the weather in China in those days. No matter how cold it was, this austerity measure was put into practice. My Chinese friends saw my difficulty and that evening when I walked out on stage to play, I noticed that they had placed two small heaters on the floor right in front of where I was to stand. I was touched, and throughout the concert I had cooking-hot feet and ice-cold fingers!

Early the next morning, many flutists and professors came to see me off. It felt like we had become a family during my brief stay. I told them I would never forget my Chinese friends. They invited me back for the following year. We hugged, and then Zhang and I left for the train station.

The Conservatory generously arranged two days in Souzhou and Hangzou for some sightseeing. I had a wonderfully relaxing stay at West Lake before leaving via China Airlines for Beijing. At the security check, a guard did not like the look of my instrument cases—especially the Alto flute case. I opened it and showed him the flute, but he still looked at me as if I was smuggling guns. He pointed to the alto flute as if to say, "Prove that you can play this thing." As I began to play, his face lit up. He motioned for me to play more. After three pieces, I was allowed to board the aircraft having almost missed my flight. Despite my late arrival I was greeted by smiling faces, some of which belonged to Chinese persons who knew just why I had been delayed!

In Beijing, I was also met by a young interpreter who was concerned he wouldn't recognize me. He stood at the flight gate waving another huge photo poster of me. The interpreter spoke five languages: Chinese, Russian, Bulgarian, Czechoslovakian, and Romanian. I speak five languages also: German, English, French, Spanish and Portuguese, but we did not have a single match between us! It seemed I would have to communicate through humor, music, and love, which are my three favorite ways to talk in any case. We had very few misunderstandings and lots of laughter. He showed me to my Beijing room. I was surprised to see it had a TV set. Television was a rare commodity in China in 1985. But, a TV set was a symbol of status. I had been honored with such a set, and it was not important whether it worked or not!

My schedule was very similar to that in Shanghai. Again, I met some fine conductors, musicians, and composers, many of whom enjoyed a childlike, joyful nature. They loved to laugh. Often after class, we got together to play trios and quartets into the night. A special highlight of my stay in Beijing was a concert for children. I started the performance with something I often do in the US for a program called "Young Audiences." I create a musical journey around the world through Europe, South America, Africa, and Asia. This seemed especially exciting for the Chinese children who had little knowledge of our Western world. Their eyes grew bigger and bigger. Then, they all stood up and played and sang for me. The Chinese start their children in musical disciplines at a very tender age. Many of my students were very accomplished.

One day after work, I heard a knocking on my door. I opened the door to find three women. They very intently repeated the same phrase over and over to me.

"Tsie, tsie han how" I replied in utter bewilderment, which means, "Thank you, very well!"

I had no idea what they wanted. Then around midnight, they arrived with a huge wooden tub, which was filled with hot water, hay and grass. They had asked if I would like a special soaking bath, and here it was! It seemed I had to strip and jump in, hay, grass, spectators and all. But, it wasn't too hard a choice given that I had been splashing myself with the cold water in my room each morning. The scene reminded me of the three ladies in Mozart's magic flute who come bearing gifts. It was definitely a highlight of my stay.

My final concert in Beijing was with a gifted string quartet that had won several international prizes. It was a pure joy to play with them. This was followed by a last and lengthy banquet when Professor Zhu, Vice President of the Conservatory and a flutist, presented me with his very precious Chinese bamboo flute which he had played from childhood. It has a hauntingly beautiful sound, which I enjoy to this day.

On my last day in China, I went to the Great Wall. There, I played two impromptu concerts. One was for a policeman who had confiscated our driver's license and only returned it after half an hour of Chinese melodies. The other was when I played for two camels. The beasts were standing on the Great Wall to provide a photo opportunity for tourists. I thought that music might bring a little diversity to their otherwise rather monotonous day. To my amazement, as soon as the music was over one of these huge animals having listened with his head tilted, came close to me and gave me a big kiss, which you can see on the cover of my album *Open Your Ears to Love*. If a camel has never kissed you, you have certainly missed something including a camel's breath! The other camel must have been a punk rock fan and obviously did not share his companion's enthusiasm for my music. He came over and bit my arm aggressively. So you see, animals have their own taste in music, too!

The next morning, I left for the airport accompanied by several favorite students. I tried to express in Chinglish, although I had learned a few phrases of Mandarin, that I'd felt at home in China because of the gift of the people's friendship, which went far beyond any barriers of culture, color, or language. We hugged, and then they waved as my flutes and I disappeared into the plane until another time.

Back in San Francisco, I rejoined Richard Patterson for more concerts in America. China had been a great experience, but my new career with Richard was in the United States as was my life with my husband Harold Ware.

# Chapter Five

# On the Road

For some six years Richard Patterson and I toured the back roads of America in a program called "Community Concerts." Richard and I shared Columbia Artists' goal to bring beautiful and uplifting music to remote areas. We met many interesting and wonderful people along the way and were stunned by their gratitude such as on one particular winter tour to sixty-five rural towns.

We were booked in a chain of small towns and some bigger cities, each spaced apart five to eight driving hours on wintry roads. At every stop—be it a community center, church hall or local school, between three hundred to a thousand eager listeners awaited us. They brought their children and in-laws to hear our music: lots of Bach and Mozart, plus our own and others' original compositions, light jazz, and some up-tempo modern-day classics.

I remember one year we played in the small, hard-bitten town of Dillon, Montana. The listeners were farmers, sheep ranchers, and laborers who eke out a living from this harsh, yet beautiful countryside. As is the case the world over, rural people are very genuine and open in their responses—much more so than city dwellers. I saw tears when we played a sad piece, and huge smiles during the light, dancing melodies.

After this concert, several of the families had pre-cooked a huge meal and brought it to a reception for us at the local Lutheran church.

They wanted to talk with Richard and me. Dillon, Montana, received us like family. They enjoyed the music immensely. It felt like a reunion of sorts—a family of those who love beauty.

Of course, there was catharsis for me, too, as I played these pieces. I sent thoughts of gratitude to my friend, Jean Michel Cousteau for his work with the dolphins, whales and the rain forest, which inspired my composition *Love Song for the Water Planet* that I recorded with Celtic harpist Kim Robertson. I also sent love to my father, dead now two years, during a piece written to celebrate his love. Richard fell into a reverie every time he played a wonderful suite on guitar that evokes "The Meadow" near his home in Half Moon Bay, California. The music buoyed us up each time we had to face another grueling day of fast food and endless driving.

At the next concert in Northern Montana, a mother brought her little boy up to the front of the stage to meet us. She had jotted down his musical commentary as he listened to our performance. The first piece was a Vivaldi concerto. The toddler had wisely noted, "That piece took a lot of practice to play." The second, more melancholy work was by Mozart. "It reminds me of Uncle," he had pronounced. The woman explained that her brother had recently died. Other music such as *Winged Dancer* reminded him of "flying in my dreams." He was so original, sensitive, and real in his feelings and reactions to the sounds. This is generally my experience. Children open themselves completely to music. As I stood meeting others after that concert, I realized the more reserved and conventional people in the audience had undergone a transformation. They were hugging each other and crying and expressed their appreciation to me with great warmth.

It always takes a little while to warm up an audience. This is especially true whenever I play in my homeland of Germany, or Europe in general. One heart-opening tool is light humor. Everyday life is so full of stress and tension. People deserve to lighten up. Richard and I tried to make our music an effective doorway to happier worlds. Even a short bout of laughter can open you to a healing from stress. Then if you let uplifting music flow in, you can soar in your mood and outlook. For this to happen, I have also found that it is crucial for the musicians' intentions to be pure. As a performer, I have to be a clear and open channel for the music so that it can then flow easily from the flute to the listener's heart. In snowy Montana, Richard and I commented on the waves of support, and sincere enthusiasm that we received from our audiences.

Ten days later, on a beautiful sunny morning, we drove from Kokomo, Indiana to Peru, Illinois. We had played nine concerts, driving seven or eight hours between gigs. My body was exhausted. But, each night, no matter how tired and achy I was, as soon as I started playing, the music healed me. For two hours, I felt completely energized. Often this lasted through the whole night.

During these long drives, we had a lot of time to prepare for the concerts, not only mentally, but also physically. It might sound like a paradox to recommend breathing to flutists. It seems that we all work a lot anyway with breathing exercises. Good breathing is one of the most essential foundations for good tone. But, I discovered that working with conscious breathing during the day improved my playing in the evenings. Not only did it improve my playing, but also it helped me to keep up my energy level during these long eight hour drives. There are many books out on breath as a tool to energize and heal the body, and breathing exercises had played a major part in my self-engendered therapy after I had broken my spine. But, I found they also helped clear my thoughts and simply made me feel better.

Some of the techniques I found especially helpful were yoga breathing and connected breathing. In connected breathing one consciously connects the inhale to the exhale without holding the breath in any part of the body.

Other exercises in the car involved control over my thoughts. When negative or unpleasant thoughts came up such as, 'This tour is so hard,' I tried to remind myself that I was the only one thinking those thoughts. Therefore, I could change my thoughts without changing anyone else's thoughts, even Richard's. So as soon as one of these negative thoughts came up I tried to replace it with a constructive thought.

In a practical way, perhaps the most powerful and simple principle is this: 'Thought is creative.' Our emotions and our physical body align and react to the thoughts that we hold. Think about being tired and you will become tired. It feels overwhelming. But, imagine that someone you really love suddenly telephones you. You become animated and discuss some of your favorite topics. The energy surges through your body and you feel refreshed.

If possible, I would also sing. Singing little songs really helped the energy, although my singing sometimes drove Richard crazy.

Through these exercises I would go from tired to wide awake, but I have to confess that often just stretching out in the back of the car is what helped most while Richard drove on wired in to sound... He had discovered Audio books!

But, traveling together on the road was never easy. I remember on one of my last Community Concert tours with Richard; my present husband was traveling with us. When Richard and I got into an argument while Peter was resting in the back seat, we were both surprised when the large round face of a stuffed bear he had bought me rose up over the front seats. "Now look," the bear said in a very deep voice. "If you two don't shut up I am going to get very upset." Richard looked at the bear and burst out laughing. Perhaps it is always a good thing to have a bear in the car as well.

As hard as it was, it was very rewarding. The best part of the touring was always meeting so many new people and playing for varied audiences of all walks of life and ages. Sometimes we had small receptions after the concerts. The locals brought cookies and punch and chatted with us. We met so many supportive people who worked hard to organize these concerts for their communities.

After the concert at Kokomo, an eleven-year-old girl came up to me her eyes sparkling as she told me how much she enjoyed the music. She had a little booklet full of sayings and poems that she'd collected from other people. She asked me to write in it. I borrowed that line from David, the young boy of eight who had written me that wonderful post scriptum to his letter: "Life is a song for the heart that is free."

I wrote the line into her book. The young girl was very moved by the saying and asked if she could whisper something in my ear. I said, "Sure."

"I've had a dream," she revealed. "In this dream, I was told I will be the first female President of the United States. I told one other person, and she laughed at me, but I still don't doubt it. If I believe in it enough, it will happen."

I told her to keep on believing. Maybe, I've already met a future President! If she follows her heart, there is no doubt she will change things for the better. Together, we talked about the secret messages of dreams and how important it is to believe in them. We hugged in parting and she promised to write.

Soon after this incident, I met a man at a truck stop who looked like a football coach. He introduced himself, "Where are you from?" he asked.

"I'm from Minnesota."

"You sound like you're from somewhere else."

"I'm originally from Germany," I replied. "I've been here twelve years and I still have an accent, but it's gotten me out of a couple of speeding tickets, so I can't complain."

He laughed, and pulled some photos from his wallet, to tell me about his beautiful young daughter. "She's a cheerleader," he said proudly.

We talked about fatherhood and I told him, "Even though my father died a couple of years ago, I still feel close to him. The love between a father and a daughter is very special. It can last forever."

All of a sudden he started to cry. He looked at me and said, "Are you a Christian?"

"Not really," I stammered. "I just believe that everything comes from the same source, and we all go back to that same source."

"As long as you believe that, you're okay," he pronounced, and we shared a moment of recognition that we all are of the same essence and that we exist in a sea of unconditional love from God.

As an assignment for myself, I worked on the idea of gratitude for fast food restaurants. They are the only ones open when Richard and I hit the road. Early in the morning and after our concerts, we were grateful for whatever was available. I have found that the simple discipline of appreciation averts much suffering. I suggested to myself that if I ate "Chicken McNuggets" with a very good attitude, they would digest better. Sometimes I even enjoyed them. Then, just when I couldn't stand another meal from *Burger King* or *McDonalds*, one of the towns we visited hosted a wonderful reception for us. The members of the Music Association in Kokomo arranged a dinner in a private home where they had all brought real food: cheesecake, dips, and meatballs.

As always, Richard and I talked to the townsfolk missing most of the food. These were great people. One family had two boys. One was very plump with an engaging smile. "I'm gonna be a comedian," he said. "I'm already one in my own family and at school." I decided that he was probably right.

His brother then piped up, "This is the first concert I have really, totally enjoyed."

What a gift! Children certainly don't pretend, so their compliments are the highest honor we can receive.

One night we were desperately trying to find something to eat after our concert. It was 11:00 p.m. by the time we got out of the hall and had packed up. We were in a small town somewhere in North Carolina and everywhere seemed closed, even *McDonalds*! Then, suddenly we saw a Greek restaurant that was still lit up inside. I immediately had the image of moussaka and delicious Greek salads and my mouth began to water. I shouted to Richard: "Let's stop! It's still open!"

"Fat chance!" Richard grumbled. "I'm sure they're closed."

But, we knocked on the door and someone opened up for us. "Sorry we just closed," the waitress informed us.

At that moment, I instantly broke out into tears. I was so completely exhausted and so desperately hungry, and I simply couldn't take another night without a nice relaxing meal. The prospect of going back to our depressing motels on an empty stomach was just overwhelming. The owner who had been standing at the counter watching this whole scene, came up and announced in his wonderful strong Greek accent: "Come in, I fix you something." And then he ran into the kitchen and started to cook us the most glorious Greek meal I had ever tasted. He brought out wine and delicious dishes and sweet baklava desserts and sat down with us while we ate and he recounted his whole life story. We celebrated warmth and friendship into the early morning hours. I will never forget that night.

The audiences had been very enthusiastic on this tour. We discovered that these local subscribers pay for four concerts each winter. Twice, people came up to us and said, "Your concert was worth the whole amount of my subscription." This is also a very nice compliment in an adult way, since many of these people had very little. They are forced to measure out even their music by money, for it's hard-won out in the farmlands.

We drove on through the Great Smoky Mountains. At concerts in this incredibly beautiful area I encountered a priest who started to cry as he said, "I felt the spirit of God in your music." A woman also claimed, "I could feel the Lord's presence in your composition, *Love Song for the Water Planet*." But, one must remember that we were touring at this time in the 'Bible Belt.'

When Richard and I returned to our respective homes for a much-needed rest before our next leg of that winter's Columbia Artists tour, I was exhausted, yet spiritually fulfilled. My experiences gave me much to reflect upon and from which to grow. I stared out of the windows of my dome-home in chilly Minnesota, grateful for home-cooked meals, warm nights in my own bed, and the joys of long hot baths.

But, all too soon Richard and I were back on the road for another five weeks for the Midwestern leg. Fortunately, we were able to begin at my home of Minneapolis and then work our way down to Del Rio, Texas, which is right on the border of Mexico. The concerts followed the same pattern—arrival in some small, or mid-sized town; a rushed visit to the concert hall, often a high school gymnasium still emanating the odors of sweat and rubber soles from the previous night's basketball game; rehearsal and a sound and light check; barely time to change into concert clothes; the concert itself, possibly followed by a reception; farewells to the caretaker of the auditorium; a quick visit to *McDonalds* or a *Burger King*; a short night in a motel and on to the next venue eight hours or more away. But, always there were the uplifting comments of our audiences to keep us going.

Occasionally, we would have to fly to the next destination in order to meet the tight schedules. We looked like we were going to miss such a flight out of San Antonio, Texas. I set our rental car flying at almost ninety miles an hour across the Texas plains. Tired and worried about our flight deadline, I missed a sign indicating an immigration checkpoint ahead. I sailed past a group of officials who emerged waving at me. At first, I waved back. Richard understood that there was something wrong regardless of our speed. "Bettine! Good grief! Stop right now!" he yelled.

I pulled over, puzzled. An official came running over to our car. "What are you doing going eighty-five miles through a stop sign?" he inquired as calmly as he could. "Are you in a hurry?"

"Yes," I replied anxiously, "We are on a concert tour trying to make our flight connection."

"Are you an American citizen?" the official asked.

Reluctantly, I admitted I was not.

"Where is your Alien Card... your Green Card?"

My stomach turned. "Well... er, it's at home," I replied. "I didn't know I had to bring it." I showed him my Minnesota driver's license as a peace offering.

He glared at me. "Do you realize I could have you put in prison for six months?"

I flushed beet red. "Dear God... No... no, I didn't know that," I stammered having no idea that I needed my Alien Card.

"Well, I'll have to check you out now. It might take half an hour to establish that you really do have a Green Card," he insisted.

Richard looked like he could kill me. We were almost certainly going to miss our flight.

The immigration officer went into his little hut while I tried to calm Richard down. After waiting a while, I decided to find out what was going on. The officer was on the phone as he was checking me out on his computer. When he was put on hold, I tried to talk to him about music and offered him one of our Christmas tapes—*An Angel's Noel.*

He accepted and his dour face relaxed. When the confirmation came through, he let me go, saying, "You must carry your Green Card at all times. You could end up in jail!"

Gratefully, I thanked him and we set out again. Miraculously, we made the plane and played that night in Athens, Texas. The sound and light crew there had marvelous 'southern' accents. During our first piece, they were working the wrong spotlights. So one of the guys yelled, "Dan, put thim lights out up yonder!" Richard and I tried to keep straight faces as we played and they continued their heavy banter. Richard had an easier task than I. It is hard to keep a good tone on the flute when you're trying not to grin. At our next stop in Tupelo, Mississippi, the school football coach was our lighting person in the gymnasium. When a lighting problem arose during rehearsal he greeted us with a rueful, "Howdy Ma'am... Sir. I downe know nothin about dem lights. I'm a coach." Fortunately, unlike in Athens, this was not actually during our performance. We reassured him it was a simple setup. Despite the spots going out at one point and a few surprising color gels, he managed. As usual, the audience seemed unaware of our problems and received us with great good will and appreciation.

"Thank you for enriching my life, ma'am," one of them said shyly after the performance.

On the road again, in Alabama I was surprised to find huge forests of colorful fall foliage as late as December. Then, we made our way up through the Great Smokies again to North Carolina, driving through forests so vast that they reminded me of the ocean. I stared ahead as I drove thinking of all my easy sea journeys, and how this was the hardest trip I had ever taken. I felt alone and tired, and in this exhausted state Richard and I were fighting with each other over silly things. But, seeing divinity in the trees I felt that necessary interconnection to sustain my spirit. The road is hard, but the rewards are worth it. We saw so much of the inspiring natural beauty of the United States.

# Chapter Six

# Young Audiences

Performing for children is particularly special. Children respond to the music in a totally all-absorbing way. For children things are black or white. They like something or they hate it, and they will react spontaneously to let you know. In many ways it is also easier for children to open their ears to love, as they are in a greater state of spiritual awareness than many adults are. The expression "age of innocence" and the Biblical quote that "out of the mouths of babes and sucklings will come greater wisdom" are observations on the reality that children are more open. They may have less mental power to reason, but their internal systems are also less cluttered by the later obstructions of mental beliefs and indoctrination that they will inevitably carry. They still feel life with their senses more than their mental capabilities and often it is easier for spontaneous Divinity to show through in their reactions and responses. Sometimes we describe the face of a child as being "full of light." How true that can be as we recognize the flow of Divinity in this light... the pure essence of the God within.

Thus, of all the roadwork I perform in the United States, performing concerts for children in a program called "Young Audiences" is for me the most rewarding. In the program, I have been invited to many schools around the country and demonstrated a variety of my flutes along with my Tibetan bells which they like to play, some of my puppet friends, which the children always like and a collection of visual images mostly of the animals that I have played for around the world.

Typically, a performance takes place in the school gymnasium or the music room, although occasionally in more expensive and better equipped schools I have found myself up on stage in a school auditorium. In reality, however, with the close bond that I like to develop with young audiences, it is far better not to be up on a stage, but close to the children at their level. It creates better participation both mentally and physically.

On one May morning in 1991, just after I had come home from a tour in South Africa, I was scheduled to give a "Young Audiences" concert for children in Central Minnesota. It was only about a two-hour drive from my home, which is unusual. Because schools are usually out in the afternoons, performances are more often scheduled in the morning at any time from 8:00 a.m. to 12 Noon, which necessitates driving to the town the day before and staying overnight in a motel much like any other road tour. This particular concert, however, was scheduled at 2:00 p.m. which time enabled me to travel there and back on the same day.

When I stepped into the school gym I was greeted with those familiar smells—sweat, cafeteria taco salad and floor varnish. Quietly, I laid out my nine flutes on a table provided, along with the puppets, my boxwood drums and Tibetan bells.

In the regular show that I perform for children the puppets have names. There is Orbit the dog, who is my travel agent, Icarus the raccoon, and my little white bear Tsie Tsie whom I brought back from China. Tsie Tsie means "Thank You" in Chinese.

I could hear the sound of children being assembled outside in the corridor, then all of a sudden the push-bar doors opened and long rows of excited children aged four to ten were marched in by young teachers and sat in orderly rows on the gym floor. The teachers to make sure that they sat down in some semblance of order had marshaled them into groups outside. There was only one male teacher on the staff. He seemed to be in charge and was always addressed as "Coach," I presume because he was the sports coach and teacher primarily in charge of the gym. When "Coach" had them all settled, I was looking at a sea of three hundred lively and curious faces.

They had such purity. I could already feel their thoughts to be filled with enthusiasm, joy and open receptivity. There was so little of the taint of preconceived opinions and prejudice in the air as with my adult audiences, who at this stage are usually wondering if my performance is going to satisfy them. I have often heard adults make comments before performance such as, "I wasn't going to come as I don't normally like flute music, but I got talked into it. I hope she's good." These are preconceived judgments. What happens to us as we grow up, to spoil the fresh state of consciousness we had in childhood?

I introduced myself by playing for them the gypsy music of Monti's *Czardas*. From the first note they reacted. Some of them giggled with surprise—the surprised joy of just hearing a sound come out of my gold flute with its many keys over the stop holes. As I swayed to the music, as is my custom in performance, some of them started swaying, too. When they imitated my movements with their arms, their teachers patiently whispered for them to sit still. But, I could see that their eyes were getting bigger and bigger as they experienced the music.

Next, I told them my name and introduced them to my flute family. I held up my gold Concert 'C' flute. "The mother," I said to their laughter. My silver alto flute I made the father; and my bass flute, which I told them "looks like a Hoover vacuum cleaner," I suggested, should be the grandfather. I held up my piccolo. "What member of the family is this?" I asked. Many hands went up and they all started shouting "Child!" Then, I heard "Baby!" I waved the piccolo in the air. "That's right! I agreed. This is the baby, and then these," I continued as I pointed out ethnic flutes from Tibet, Peru, Greece and China, "are the baby's brothers and sisters." Now, they were all laughing.

To involve them in the process of making music, I then asked them: "What do you think I have to do to get a sound out of this flute?" Many of them again eagerly raised their hands and shouted out, "Blow!"

I blew very hard into the flute. Absolutely no sound came out. "What happened?" I asked feigning surprise.

"You have to push the buttons," a fat boy in the front row yelled. So I blew and pressed the keys, but still nothing happened.

"You have to suck the air in," a Scandinavian-looking girl with long plaits suggested.

"Maybe it's not plugged in," an older boy from the back chimed in.

They then all started yelling suggestions: "Try humming!" or "It's broken!" until a serious-looking kid with glasses shouted, "You have to blow over it." I blew across the mouthpiece and beautiful notes started to come out. The children quieted down absorbed by the miracle of the sound.

There was a big map on the wall, which I had requested. I told the children that I had just been in Africa and pointed it out to them. Now, it was time for them to meet my traveling companions—the puppets. I told the children that a week ago I had been walking in the park when I heard these strange voices. I then pulled out Tsie Tsie the bear and Orbit the dog.

"What should we do for these children we're going to play for in Minnesota?" I made Tsie Tsie ask in a polite bear voice.

Orbit responded with a deep gruff voice: "How about we take them around the world with music?"

"Yes! Yes!" cried Tsie Tsie. "Then they can see what we see as we go to all the different countries to play music."

At this point I needed two volunteers, but when I asked, every child in the room put up their hands and shouted "Me! Me!" Eventually, I settled on two gregarious kids, if possible a boy and a girl, and told them they were to be our pilot and flight attendant on this journey around the world. Then, we learned a few words of Italian together to prepare us for Italy.

"Fasten your seat belts!" I shouted. "We are off to Venice!"

This seemed to ring a bell with the children. It would seem that every one of them must have already flown or been well-trained in the back seat of the car, which is something of a reflection on how much we travel today, even if it is just within our own country. All the children knew how to go through the motions of fastening seat belts.

"I'm going to play some music from Italy," I informed them. "I'm going to pick a season. It will be spring, summer, fall or winter, but I'm not going to tell you which one. I want you to guess." I then played a section from Vivaldi's *Four Seasons*.

The younger they were the more accurate seemed their guesses, many shouting out "Spring!"

I asked them how they could tell.

"It sounded like birds singing," many of them suggested.

I then asked our pilot to take us to Austria and we all fastened our seat belts again. For Austria I told the children about a composer who was born many years ago in Salzburg. "He is very famous," I hinted, "and he began to play and write music when he was even smaller than some of you. Raise your hand if you know his name."

Response was slower to this question. I then tried to help them by saying that they made a movie about him.

"Elvis Presley!" the chubby boy in the front yelled. I laughed, but assured him that he wasn't far off as Elvis Presley was indeed very famous, he had once lived in Germany which is close to Austria, and they did make a movie about him, but the composer I had in mind had lived rather longer ago. Eventually, aided in part by an over-enthusiastic music teacher, somebody shouted "Mozart!" but not before another child had suggested "God."

Next stop was Norway for which country I demonstrated the Selje floete. I had set up my echo machine, which is just a pedal on the floor, but the children didn't know it. I started to play a traditional Norwegian shepherd's song. It sounded as if I was playing in the high mountains where there were many sheep and beautiful green meadows. "If you listen very closely," I suggested, "you might even hear a surprise." I pressed the pedal for the echo and it sounded like three or four different flutes had joined in.

After the Norwegian piece I asked them: "Did you hear that echo?" They all had. "Where did you think it came from?"

"The flute!" many shouted.

I played the same flute for them, but it made no echo.

"It came because we were in the mountains," a thin, dreamy-looking girl suggested.

How wondrous, I thought. Children's imagination is still working so well. She really did go to the mountains.

Finally, one of them in the front row who had seen me press the foot pedal spilled the beans: "That thing that you pressed the button on."

We continued our journey around the world in this way stopping in China where I got a rather self-conscious young lady named Sarah to play the Tibetan bells for me. She did pretty well, only missing them once to the delight of her classmates while I played both my Tibetan flute and one of the Chinese flutes that had been given to me when I was teaching those Master Classes in Shanghai. We also traveled to Brazil, Ireland and Greece. Every time I would point out where we were going on the big map and occasionally Orbit and Tsie Tsie would add words of wisdom. At one point Orbit and Icarus the raccoon, got into a fight because Icarus complained that Orbit had given him the wrong tickets. When the raccoon hit Orbit over the head and told him he was "Stupid!" there were peels of laughter from the children.

Finally, I performed an arrangement of *Talk to the Animals* from the movie *Dr. Doolittle* to a slide presentation of animals that I have played for around the world. There were many Australian animals— koala bears, emus, wombats, kangaroos, dingoes and Tasmanian devils, I also showed them horses from Ireland, along with dogs and cats. There were camels from Egypt and monkeys and jungle animals from Brazil including spiders. Most important of all was the original slide taken in China that is the cover sleeve for my CD of the same name as this book—*Open your Ears to Love*. It is of the camel kissing me on the Great Wall of China. It was almost impossible to hear the music, because when each animal came up on the screen there was such a spontaneous and joyous response from the children. "Emu!" they shouted, or "Tazzie Devil!" It amazed me what a good knowledge of our planet's fauna these children had. But, they had their opinions. They loved a cat poking through a restaurant railing in Greece, and physically rejected the spider in the Brazilian jungle.

At the end, I encouraged the children to ask any questions they might have about the music, the flutes, or being a musician. Many hands flew up. I called on a sweet-looking girl in the second row. She shyly said: "My Grandmother also once went to Mexico." I thanked her for her comment and called on an impish boy sitting at the back. "I got my tooth out today," he announced. I felt the love that came from these children, as they simply wanted to share something from their life with me. But, now I got the serious questions. "What do these flutes cost?" "Are you married?" "How old are you?" "Where did you get the money to buy these flutes?" I answered with good-sported humor. One kid even asked, "What is the meaning of life?"

"For me," I answered, "life is about learning how to give love and joy to others." The little boy nodded in agreement with this reply.

Then, the group gave a big round of applause to the pilot and flight attendant and the shy Tibetan bell player, and I told them they could all come up to meet my family. This was a mistake: they ran up wildly wanting to touch the flutes and try to make sounds themselves, but with their teachers' help I controlled their curiosity.

So many of the children I meet are already inspired by the idea of playing music. My job is just to give them scope and room for their imagination, as they dream of ways to give to themselves and others through music.

Over the years in the "Young Audiences" program and individually through school concerts I must have played for over 350,000 children. Hopefully I have opened their ears to love through my performances, they have certainly opened my ears to love as I have sensed their uninhibited inner spirituality come through in their spontaneity of response.

"To heights and depths no words can reach ... Music is the soul's own speech."

# Chapter Seven

# *Healing Hard Times*

It was Christmas Eve, 1989. The temperature outside had plummeted to thirty degrees below zero. I sat gazing out over a dark Minnesota lake, feeling numb. Just three days before, I had left my husband of ten years and moved into a small cabin. It had started to hit me. I felt very alone and cold. The cabin didn't have proper insulation, if any, under its raised wooden floor. The cold seeped up from below those boards.

Questions raced through my mind. 'Did I make the right decision?' And yet for almost two years things had been strained. Harold and I had both been nudged to move forward, to move on with our lives. It was best to separate in friendship. I felt enormous sadness, resentment, and most of all guilt. I believed in marriage. One shouldn't have failed like this morally or spiritually. I had let myself down. I wavered constantly between repressing the shame and pain, and letting it out in hot tears. Divorce was considered a big failure in my family. I hadn't even told my parents in Germany yet. I dreaded their reaction. They might not even want to take me into their hearts and offer support.

During the coming months, I took many walks on frozen Medicine Lake, just a block away from my new home. I reflected on my marriage, which had been mostly filled with love. But, there had always been a problem: I depended on another for worthiness and love. I felt I must now learn how to rely on myself for approval and accept myself as I am. Nature quietly provided a healing balm, as I sifted down to the truth. Beautiful sunsets from my window highlighted the serenity of winter. But, I easily reverted back into complete self-pity.

'I might as well take the time to really look at myself,' I thought. An unswerving self-inventory was called for. For months I hardly spoke to anyone. Many wounded feelings from my childhood and teenage years bubbled to the surface. But, in a way this was a gift, a true opportunity to assess where I was in life.

For the first time, I discovered the precious value of women friends. What wonderful support we gave to each other! Each of my friends, who were used to seeing me come and go, were now so willing to support me and listen to my grief. They took me out for a movie and afterward, a cup of tea.

My ex-husband was still very considerate. He came over to help me with the car and the many details of sorting out our lives. One day I tried to numb myself with wine. I was driving home, but I should have called a cab. I saw Harold coming from the opposite direction and we both pulled over. He embraced me and gave me encouragement. I knew he would always love me.

I vaguely started to correlate my beliefs with my experiences. 'What belief is behind this creation?' I asked. It required complete, excruciating honesty. We cannot blame another for what happens in our lives. Sometimes it's a co-creation, like a marriage, but we agree to these collaborations. In almost every life, bad things happen that we can't anticipate. But, we can choose our reaction to them. If a fire were to break out on a ship on which I was sailing, I could still think about what is important in my life. Even if I was to die, I know I would continue to exist in some other energy. I still can choose where my attention goes in each moment. Is it to be something uplifting, the music of life, or something dark that creates more darkness to come?

But, as I reflected on my failed marriage, this time at Medicine Lake seemed the darkest time of all. Looking back, I could remember other hard times—events like my car accident at age sixteen or my broken back seven years later when I was thrown from that horse. Did I choose from the higher viewpoint of soul for even these events to happen? After all, they did turn out to be blessings. I got to glimpse higher realities through them. My "near-death experience" in the accident showed me that there is no spiritual death, and breaking my spine at age twenty-four taught me to rely on my inner strength and awareness. It provided much-needed quietness to explore what was really inside me.

In my grief after divorce, however, I hit rock bottom. I had no concert bookings. I had no energy, and my health was suffering. I decided I had a choice here: I could continue to bathe in my misery, or I could start to work myself out of this dark night of soul. Maybe this blow had been much needed in order to force me to create a change.

I started to experiment with many types of spiritual healing: rebirthing, massage, chiropractic adjustments, tai chi, and circular breathing. I discovered that if I made time for just twenty so-called "connected breaths," linking the in-breath to one's out-breath, it made me feel better immediately. This is such a simple exercise since we breathe all the time, but it really relieves stress. I wanted to tell everyone: "You are always only one breath away from change."

Humor is essential. In some of those darkest hours, especially at night, I went to the video store to rent comedies. I especially liked those old British ones like *Fawlty Towers*, or *Are You Being Served?* They carried me from sad tears to laughter.

I also read many books on healing and meditation. When I was in the darkest, darkest time, I sang myself to sleep.

On cold nights when I was shivering in my bed, which was only a mattress on the floor above those draughty boards, I remember singing my favorite name for God, "Hu." A very gentle, sweet music started in my inner ear. It filled my heart, and caressed it with a simple message: "I am loved and accepted. I am not a failure. I am God's music, too."

I began to step outside of my fixed attention on my misery. It's hard to let in new, creative projects. I just concentrated on taking baby steps. But, I was amazed. Every time I opened my heart even a little, things began to leap forward.

Suffering is definitely not the only way to learn. I decided to be more proactive in the future. If I saw a change was needed to be made for growth, I would leap at it. I discovered more and more the close relationship between my beliefs and my experiences, and how much freedom I had in the choice of my thoughts and moods. I got glimpses of the tremendous power that lies within us—power to create and sculpt our lives deliberately.

Out of the blue, I got a call from one of the cruise lines I had worked with in the past: "Can you play on a three-week cruise from Alaska to Japan?" I accepted with relief. What a most welcome gift! I would be playing again. I put all my feelings into the music. I realized that when the sound flows through my body and emotions, it drains the poison and frees the divine energy of my soul. I started breathing again. The life force started to seep back into me.

I chatted with people on the ship, slowly emerging from my self-created hibernation. I was like a bear waking up after a long, long winter. In fact, during my depression a friend had given me a stuffed bear to cheer me up. He was a good companion. Little did I know that he was just the first in a huge collection, the beginning of a long and intense love affair I have had and still have with bears. They say the world is divided into two kinds of people: "Those who love teddy bears and those who don't. And neither understands the other."

My bear family, which started in those darkest of times, now extends to seventy or eighty stuffed animals. My present husband, Peter, and I often talk to each other through these bears. It helps us defuse arguments and get our true feelings out. Sometimes the bears even start talking for themselves! They all have different names and tasks. Bigfoot is a real Minnesotan. He takes care of the house and the cars. Caramel Bear is our healing bear. When Peter hurt his back and had to lie flat for ten days, Caramel Bear accompanied him. Webster is an adorable bear who stutters and finds it hard to make a complete sentence, which is very frustrating for a relative of the man who wrote the dictionary! Dr. Crow looks like a relative of Heckel and Jekyl, and thinks that because in Native American folklore his relatives bring wisdom and are at the top of the totem pole, that he is more intelligent than the bears. But, he has a good heart and tends to get over-excited which makes him endearing. Then, there is 'K Mart' Bear who was awarded a watch for long time service in the famed chain stores. He is almost more earnest than Dr. Crow and thinks that everything can be sold at bargain basement prices... the blue light special! Finally, there is Initiate Bear who thinks that he is more spiritual than the others are. He is a bit preachy. He tries to instruct the other bears in spiritual practices, but they usually ignore him and often show more spirituality in their loving characters than by adhering to Initiate's path.

As Peter is also often at sea, about seven to nine bears travel with us around the world. Half go with Peter, who was the Cruise Director for the *Queen Elizabeth 2* for seven years, and now lectures on board ships, and half go adventuring with me. Bacpac is a regular traveler in my entourage. He is an ambassador from the bear world to cultures around the globe. All of us have great reunions when we meet again in foreign ports and distant lands. The bears sometimes run up big phone bills keeping in touch. They provide humor in the midst of heated arguments. If things get too bad, they cut in to remind us how silly we are, or call a bear convention to help resolve a serious problem in the household. On such occasions we often end up in laughter and the problem recedes.

Peter and I say we could never separate, because the bears would never get over it. But reflecting back on my experience, hard and dark times come for everyone. Don't fight them. They offer a great opportunity to really know oneself, to grow, and to change. You find out what is really true for you, and who your real friends are. Perforce, you discover new tools that can lift you in creativity and mood and you often go on to a different and better life. I am happier now than I've ever been. Yes, there is happiness even after life has dealt you its worst blows.

What did my divorce teach me? It taught me not to sweep bad feelings under the rug. You must talk and let them out. If you can't feel and own your feelings, you can't change them, and you can't live an honest, productive life.

Now, I sometimes let myself dive into anger and sadness... not to wallow or be destructive, but just to really own my feeling, recognize it for what it is, and then create something better. And I completely accept that I create all my feelings. As a result I believe I have much more compassion for others now after going through separation, divorce, and the death of a loved one. I've been there. I let my feelings act as a compass, pointing me to my true path. I try to discriminate more in my thoughts and choices, and really take responsibility for my state of consciousness. If it doesn't feel right, it's not right. I have tried to stop judging others and no longer hold so many rigid opinions. Everything is our own creation... an expression of our Divine power, our higher consciousness.

Naturally, this hard-won wisdom has brought me more freedom and joy. I am constantly filled with the excitement of creating the reality that I choose. I listen to my feelings, good and bad, and let my heart lead me, no matter how difficult the path.

We create our own reality all the time. Usually we do it unconsciously. We manifest our doubts and fears, instead of our fondest wishes. Now, I try to live out my biggest, best dreams and focus upon them—I have found my own internal power.

# Chapter Eight

# A Sad Farewell and a New Beginning

**M**y father's death hit me hard. It was the second time I'd lost someone close. His death was a surprise. He had always been pretty healthy and had been admitted to the hospital for a routine operation and was expected to make a good recovery. Instead, he died. When I received the phone call from Germany that he had slipped into a coma, I flew to his bedside.

I barely recognized him, he looked so different. I sat by his bed and thanked him for being my father. I told him what was going on in my life. I shared the pain of my separation from Harold. He didn't respond outwardly, but I felt a great peace the night he died, as if his whole beingness had enveloped me like a warm cloak of love. He was comforting me not I him. He showed me that he was in a very elated state.

It was one of my father's greatest joys that I became a musician. He himself loved to play the violin, although his first calling was as a teacher and Shakespearean scholar. Our relationship was interesting. When I was a child, he was always away working. I hardly knew him and when he was home he just wanted us to keep quiet. But, during my convalescence from the car accident that killed my boyfriend when I was sixteen, we got to know each other better and I learned of this great man's beauty and love. Others could see this instantly in his radiant eyes, but I suppose as a child I was too close to him to appreciate

57

this. When we found each other, however, a loving friendship developed that lasted until he died. When I would come over from the United States and visit him in Germany it was the high point of his year. He canceled all his other activities and commitments to spend time walking with me in the forests around our family home. But, the first thing we would always do was to play duets together on the violin and flute. That joy set the tone for our conversations. He originally wanted me to be solely a classical musician, so when I branched out into more contemporary concerts, I worried I would disappoint him. But, I had no reason to fear. He always stood by me encouraging me in my career. When he died, I felt nobody would ever love me in such an unconditional way again. I remember a special moment at his funeral. Just when the casket was being lowered into the ground, a bird began singing jubilantly in a nearby tree. Everybody caught their breath at the beauty of it. I felt my father's spirit exulting, "I'm not down there. I'm free!"

At that moment, my heart opened wider through the pain of loss, instead of contracting. Everyone I met evoked more compassion and love in me. It reminded me that life is short. I loved my father very much—his company, the shared music and his care. He taught me to appreciate the moment, to be more tolerant and to enjoy people as they are.

Later that month, the University in Munich held a memorial celebration in honor of my father. I was quite surprised to see thousands of people there. He had touched many lives. I played some music I'd written for his eightieth birthday. I tried to talk about him and played three movements that I felt expressed his qualities: Tolerance, Humor, and Unconditional Love. The other speakers were very somber, but I felt his presence lift me as I spoke, giving encouragement. Death is only sad for those who are left behind.

After my father's death, I became really close to my mother, probably for the first time in my life. We had always had rather a difficult relationship up until then. Mostly, I had resented her for being so ascetic and unfeminine and I had rebelled all my life fearing that I might become like her. Now, however, I felt sincere love and compassion with her and we discovered each other in a deeper way. I came home more often to be with "her" and also with my two brothers. We all had to help each other now as the strong center and anchor of our family had left.

Many times I have felt my father's presence like a guardian angel. My father is there, watching over me. I even feel he led me to my current husband, Peter. It's something I can't put into words, but shortly after my father's death, Peter and I met. Perhaps it just remains associated in my mind, or maybe it was the spirit of my father who led me to the *Queen Elizabeth 2* for some special concerts, which began a wonderful romance.

When I was living alone in that little hut out by Medicine Lake in Minnesota after Harold and I had separated, Zanna, one of my girlfriends, visited me. "I had a dream about you last night," she said excitedly as she boiled up some hot water for tea. "I dreamed that I was at your wedding."

"What do you mean?" I asked as I reflected back on the happy day that Harold and I had got married at sunrise on a California hillside.

"You got married to a man named Peter David Longley. We were all at your wedding," Zanna continued.

"But I don't know anyone of that name," I cried out in frustration. "Besides, I might not like the guy!"

Five years later, shortly after my father had died, I was invited to play these concerts on board the Cunard flagship *Queen Elizabeth 2* more popularly known as the *QE2*. The ship was on her annual World Cruise and had reached Mombassa on the east coast of Africa. I traveled to the ship with guitarist Barbara Polasek, my German counterpart to Richard Patterson. We were engaged as a classical duo. It was hot and humid and we had been traveling long hours. Leaving our baggage at the foot of the gangway we were escorted on board to meet the Cruise Director. Can you imagine what I felt when I learned his name was Peter Hovenden Longley!

Peter was dark and handsome; a suave Englishman who was much loved by the other entertainers on board the *QE2*. He seemed a little shy and rather formal as he shook our hands, but I could tell that he was a kind and thoughtful person when he immediately offered to carry our bags up from the gangway to our cabin. In my experience, no Cruise Director on any other ship had offered to carry my bags.

Naturally, I was curious about Peter, even if his middle name did not match that in Zanna's dream. 'Two names out of three,' I reasoned was pretty darned accurate. But, he was somewhat inaccessible. He seemed shy, and although he was always polite, he didn't say much more to me until after I had played my final concert. In fact, Barbara told me to forget about him. She thought he was gay. We had performed in the Grand Lounge, which was unusual for classical performers. I had played my composition *Love Song for the Water Planet* to Kim Robertson's harp track and the sound of tropical birds in the rain forest. Peter came backstage after the show and simply said, "We've got to talk."

Talk we did. He was deeply moved by my music and it had sparked in him a spiritual response, which led him to share his remarkable story with me. He was writing an immense historical novel on the life and times of Jesus and Mary Magdalene encompassing a very different interpretation of Jesus' message to the world than that which has been handed down to us in Christianity. I was leaving the ship the next day in Freetown, Sierra Leone, West Africa. I don't recommend that anyone should ever have to leave a ship in Freetown, but that is another story. Peter and I sat up in the ship's nightclub most of that night and he shared incredible passages with me from his remarkable book. We found we were spiritually in tune with each other.

I did not see Peter again for nearly twelve months, not until I traveled on the *QE2* during her World Cruise the following year. I had sent him several letters and received back four cards all posted at the same time none of which I could read. If Peter did not type his manuscripts nobody would ever be able to decipher his work, and yet strangely enough this man is among many other things a teacher of calligraphy! I was traveling with Kim Robertson that winter. We both took Peter's calligraphy class, although I have to admit my reasons had little to do with learning the art. But, as I learned, calligraphy is an art form and is in no way related to handwriting. Peter communicates with his art form, but certainly not with his handwriting.

Our relationship developed somewhat further during this voyage, still very much centered on our spiritual discussions, but certainly revealing more intimate interests. It did not look, however, that we would come together even though we both felt this strong love that came from a deep spiritual recognition. I felt I had known Peter for ages. He had told me that he was still in a twelve-year relationship with a Japanese woman who has since become a dear friend of mine, too, and that he simply could not separate from her. It looked like we would perhaps not see each other again. My heart hurt as I recalled Zanna's dream and felt the loss of this possible future, but somewhere deep within I always knew that I would love Peter unconditionally. It took an accident at sea to finally bring us together.

Wanting to express that love, I composed a piece for Peter, *Total Freedom in Divine Love*, which I later renamed *Forever*. I really thought that this was the end of our relationship at the time, but I wanted to express my spiritual bonding with him in this way. Two weeks after I had sent him the tape, the *QE2* sailed into some uncharted granite rocks off Martha's Vineyard. The date was August 7th, 1992, and I was in Germany on a concert tour.

That night I had a strange dream. I saw Peter on board the QE2 all covered in mud and lining up the passengers for a masquerade parade. The ship looked like it had been dredged up from the bottom of the ocean. Then, Barbara Polasek called me.

"Have you seen the news?" she asked and before I could answer continued in an excited way: "The *QE2* has had an accident and she's sinking!"

My heart sank. 'Was Peter all right?'

Two days later, I checked my messages from Germany. Peter had left several messages on my machine in Minnesota telling me about the accident, but that everything was fine and that he was now stuck in Boston for a month while the ship was to be repaired. "If you are in the country at all," he said, "Give me a call. At least we can talk."

A window had opened and with all the synchronicity that now seemed to surround our relationship, I made a momentous decision that changed my life. I faxed the *QE2* in Boston and told Peter that I had a concert at the Festival Hall in London the following week, but that I would fly to London from Munich via Boston. I did, and that decision led to us getting engaged the following month and married the next year. I have always said that we are probably the only couple that can honestly say that our marriage "started on the rocks." It can only go uphill from there!

Peter proposed in a Minnesota meadow when we were driving home from a visit to the North Shore of Lake Superior. The sun was setting and a full moon was rising. In the old fashioned way he proposed on bended knee. Naturally, I said, "Yes." It was only then, that I told him about Zanna's dream. To this day that dream is recorded in her Dream Journal.

We had an official engagement party on board the *QE2* on the World Cruise in February 1993. I was traveling with Kim Robertson again and we were journeying around South America. The following June, Peter and I were married in the little dome house in Minnesota that was my father's last and most generous gift to me. The ceremony was meant to be in the garden which masterfully Peter had created almost overnight. But, it poured with rain, and instead the ceremony was in the garage. Peter is a painter as well as a calligrapher, and his paintings adorned the walls while Sam's Club carpets covered the floor. Huge arrangements of flowers completed the scene and Kim provided the music. Apart from Peter's two sisters the only family member at our wedding was my beloved ex-husband, Harold Ware. How happy I was for him three years later when we attended his second wedding and Peter arranged the flowers and I played the music.

Although Peter and I were officially married in Minnesota, just over two weeks later we went through a second ceremony in an Anglican church in England in which his mother and father had been married fifty-three years before. This was for our European relatives to attend. My brother Harald came over to England with an Uncle and Aunt from Germany, but my mother did not feel she could make the journey.

Peter had met my mother the previous winter when we had gone over to England for Christmas celebrations with his family. After Christmas we flew to Munich to visit my mother at Endorf. The old family home looked at its best in sparkling white frost that hung in great garlands from the trees with a clear view across to the Bavarian Alps. We decided to visit her again on our honeymoon.

We arrived with our arms full of pictures and even a video of our British nuptials. I was a little shocked to see her so tired. She spoke unrelentingly of leaving this world. I didn't want to listen, even though she was eighty-three. My father had been gone now for three years, and she said she was ready to join him.

She told me how important and joyful it was to see me so happy. Her life was now complete. But, despite the joy, it was a very difficult week. Three different incidents arose and I became very impatient, which is unusual for me. I put it down to the stress of all the wedding planning. I have much respect for people who survive a large wedding. My first wedding was very informal, celebrated with a quiet potluck dinner among friends. Peter and I had many more people to consider for my second and his first marriage. Both ceremonies involved accommodating friends, holding receptions, and much detailed planning. So I was exhausted when I saw my mother. But deep inside, I may have known it was the last time I would see her.

I was scared, and it seemed like we had a deeper agenda. Everything unspoken between us came up and had to be worked out. I was a bit disappointed in my performance. When she asked to see the wedding photos yet again, I was exasperated. "You've seen them three times!" I yelled. Everything she did seemed to irritate me.

But, before we returned home to the US, she wrote Peter a letter in English. It read: "I am so very very glad and thankful to have seen you here in this world before I go into the higher world and to know how good it is for Bettine to have found you and will be connected with you in the light of Christus." I didn't know what to say. She cried when we parted—the only time I can remember her doing so in this life—even when my father died she did not cry! My mother prided herself on being a very controlled, composed person.

I spoke to my mother on the telephone several times after I returned to the US. The last time, she called to say she'd opened some of my financial mail. I exploded, yelling at her over the phone, "Don't ever do that, put it away." I slammed down the receiver, filled with anger. I didn't call her back, even though my inner voice nudged me to make it right.

One afternoon about three weeks after our return to the US, my friend Kim Robertson, the harpist, came over to rehearse for a special concert. Ironically, we were planning to perform it for my mother in Endorf, Germany that Fall. Then, the phone rang. It was my brother. He sobbingly told me that my mother was dead. She'd had an accident in her car. They drive so fast in Germany. The medics had airlifted her to a hospital via helicopter, but she had died shortly thereafter.

The bitter words burned in my brain. I'd never felt such pain and desperation or so lost. I had lashed out at her during my last communication... hung up on her, even though I had said many times how much I loved her.

I was ripped apart, but nonetheless consoled by the fact that my beloved Peter left the *QE2* in the Bahamas to fly back to Minnesota and accompany me to Germany for the funeral. At my mother's funeral, I played her favorite Bach concerto, which helped me a little. When I finished, a calm slipped over me. I sensed... even knew that she was all right. In fact, my heart felt that she had been released from this world into a wonderful journey. Peter sensed her presence after the funeral when he felt he saw her looking down at us from an old tree in the courtyard of my brother's home. He said she looked serene, rather like the Cheshire Cat in Lewis Carroll's *Alice in Wonderland*. Momentarily, I felt her joy and I believe that she was with my father.

Still, the pain in my heart persisted. I was disappointed in myself, and so much more alone in a world without either of my parents. After two months I couldn't bear it anymore. I wrote a letter to my spiritual guide and teacher of Eckankar, Harold Klemp, and asked him for help.

Whether my mother's spirit picked up the energy of that letter or not I will never know, but that night a miracle occurred, a miracle of healing. I fell into a deep dream. In this dream, I saw my parents sitting together in a boat on a beautiful lake in Europe. They were once again in youthful love. Father had long, wavy hair and wore a leather jacket. Mother looked equally young and beautiful. Slowly, she turned and came to me. "Bettine, don't be sad," she said. "I had to leave so suddenly because my memory loss was getting worse. I didn't want to live like that. Forgive me. Everything is all right. You have nothing to feel bad about. I love you." Then, in my dream state she hugged me, and when I awoke I could feel her love and her touch.

With her benediction on my lips, I awoke. My face streamed with tears of relief as I wrote the dream down in my journal. The guilt was lifted. She knew I loved her, which was the most important thing. I could go on with life.

This experience taught me an important lesson. It is never too late to mend old wounds, to heal old hurts, and to make things right, even if the others involved are gone from this world. Even when you feel you have completely failed in the most important moments of your life, it is possible to repair those feelings. You may despair of such a gift, but I believe there is always a way. In my case, it came through a dream, much as it had in Brazil many years before when my beloved dog friend Cyril taught me a similar lesson—a spiritual gift of healing.

I was so grateful, for even though I couldn't make things right here in the physical world between my mother and me, my heart was able to receive her love. There was still an inner connection, and that allowed me to communicate through the mysterious music of dreams.

# Chapter Nine

# Surprise in the Sauna

I started to play concerts on ships while touring with Richard Patterson. Ironically, in those days I even sailed on ships of the Royal Viking Line while Peter was Cruise Director of the *Royal Viking Star*, but we never met. I guess Richard and I must have always sailed on the *Royal Viking Sea* or the *Royal Viking Sky*. After I married Peter I started to travel even more at sea. I had created a shipboard cabaret and multi-media show, which led ultimately to my giving up my tours with Richard. I then found myself touring extensively around the world, and not just in the conventional cruising areas that Richard and I had explored in the Caribbean, the Norwegian fjords and Alaska.

Life at sea is hectic in its own way. Rehearsals have to be scheduled at times when passengers are not using relevant public rooms. This generally means at night, but a ship at sea during the night has its own rhythm.

I had been rehearsing with the Polish band on board one of these ships. The rehearsal finally ended at 3:00 a.m. Eight young singers and dancers immediately started practicing for their evening show. They couldn't wait for me to be finished so that they could have the stage. They probably then rehearsed until about 5:00 a.m.

Wearily I packed up all my flutes and dragged my flute bag below decks to my cabin. Then, I decided to take a walk through the sleeping ship. Everywhere was quiet except in the ballroom, where the Filipino night cleaners were vacuuming the carpets. The ship was a peaceful encapsulated hotel, adrift on the high seas.

Out on deck the warm Caribbean air felt like wet velvet. A full moon greeted me as I stood gazing at its glittering reflection on the water. Space... there is nothing but open space wherever one turns on the ocean. It is the closest I ever feel to realizing or being in the inner space of the soul. The water and sky evoke the memory of my true home.

'Tomorrow will be another sea day,' I mused. I love the days at sea. I spend many hours "walking on the water," which is how one describes taking endless turns around the promenade deck. I love to breathe in the delicious, pure sea air, and feast on the sights and sounds of the ocean surrounding us. I often have to pause and send thanks to life for being able to earn my living in this exciting way. But, of all the experiences on board ship, it is the people one meets that often leave the greatest impression.

The next day, several hours before my evening show, which was scheduled in the Grand Ballroom, I went into the sauna to relax. Only one older woman was there. She was naked like me and after a few minutes of silence she addressed me in a strong German accent: "You must be European, because the Americans always come dressed in bathing suits, even sweats, and at least a towel."

"How right you are," I answered. "I've felt embarrassed at times sitting in the nude between all the dressed Americans. But, coming from Europe, it really seems crazy to have wet clothes hampering the cleansing process."

The German lady turned out to be quite talkative. Pretty soon she was telling me a striking story about her nephew, who at eighteen, developed a strong affinity for the Buddhist way of life. "We always found him to be rather strange," she told me with a growing intensity in spite of all the sweating. "Then, he met these people from Tibet and went with them to the Himalayas. There, he was introduced to the work of a Tibetan lama who died 200 years ago. Well, he became a lama himself and finished the writings of that lama exactly where the man had left off before he died. That book is now known as *The Way of the White Clouds*. The author is listed as Govinda—that's my nephew. He believes he was this former lama 200 years ago in a previous life."

"What a great story," I told her sweating so hard that I could hardly breathe. "But, I'm afraid I've overstayed my time in this intense heat.

I can feel my heart racing, but for a story like that the discomfort is worth it."

That evening, this same German lady I had met in the sauna came up to me after my show. Of course, we both looked quite different now in formal, beaded dresses, make-up and groomed hair, but we recognized each other. I thanked her again for sharing her wonderful story about reincarnation in the sauna. I know I will never forget her nephew's story. And, when I read *The Way of the White Clouds* again (a very famous Buddhist text today) it will now have a very personal and special ring for me. We hugged each other and said "Goodnight."

Before I fell asleep that night, I thought about the events of the day. Then, I recalled another sauna encounter. It was a few years earlier on a different ship. Again, I was lying on a towel sweating on the top shelf of the sauna. Suddenly, the door opened and in came a very short, older lady, also in the nude. She sat down on the lower shelf without realizing there was someone else in the sauna. After several minutes of cooking in silence I felt compelled to let her know I was there, so she wouldn't be startled. I offered something weak, such as, "It sure is hot in here!" which is really quite a stupid thing to say in a sauna.

The older lady almost catapulted from her seat, startled by the fact that she had not been alone. She shouted in one of the strongest German accents that I had ever heard: "Where does this German accent come from?"

At that moment I recognized who this lady was. It was Dr. Ruth Westheimer, the world's most famous sex therapist. And here I was meeting her in the sauna without any clothes on! We had a great time chatting, not only then, but also throughout the whole two-week cruise during which she gave several very direct lectures as our celebrity guest.

The themes ranged from "How to Improve your Sex Life," which of course seemed very urgent for the many eighty-year-old passengers, to "Sexual Illiteracy Exposed," which met the interests of younger people. Dr. Westheimer is very short. She's only four foot nine inches or so and one can barely see her when she first comes on to the stage hidden behind the podium. But, when she grabs the microphone and makes her opening statement in that strong German accent of hers, she catches everyone's attention: "The first thing I want to tell you," she says, "is size doesn't matter!" With her charismatic and enthusiastic style, Dr. Westheimer won almost everybody's heart. We became good friends and she revealed her amazing story of having lost everything in the holocaust.

'How many interesting teachers both of this life and in past reincarnations can one hear about in the sauna,' I thought, before sleep finally took over.

# Chapter Ten

# Mediterranean Experiences

One Spring I found myself cruising in the Mediterranean. At that time of the year the sea is still cold, but the March air is filled with a clean, invigorating tang. Our voyage promised all the famed romance of a combined visit to the ancient ruins of Greece and Egypt. This was the world of Pericles, Aristotle, Alexander the Great, Cleopatra, Mark Anthony and Augustus Caesar.

My journey brought me first to Alexandria, ancient center of science and learning. Ptolemy kept the world's greatest archive of scrolls here. In the famed library built in 300 BC was catalogued the philosophy, art, literature, and science of the Ancient world. Then, the library caught fire and much of the world's wisdom and history was destroyed. So it became necessary for a new cycle of discovery. How many times must we reinvent the wheel in our long history of spiritual striving?

Modern Alexandria bears little evidence of its glorious past. I had last been there about four years before and I could still remember the unbelievable smells and the shrieking traffic, which seemed to follow no rules other than those that Egyptians invent. At every corner, aggressive merchants tried to pull me into dark shops with inflated prices. Beggars dogged our footsteps with piteous pleas for money. This is not a comfortable city. But, I also recalled a magical visit to one of the ancient mosques. There, I had a very special encounter with two mullahs, or high priests of the Moslem faith.

As our ship's tender came toward the dock, I wondered on this beautiful morning if those mullahs were still at the same mosque. I suggested to my friend Liz that maybe we should find out. Immediately after we stepped off the tender onto the dock we were instantly surrounded by at least fifteen shouting Egyptians—merchants, beggars, taxi drivers, and horse and buggy owners. "No... no! No carpets... No jewelry! No T-shirts, not now!" we shouted. None of them had any qualms about accosting our privacy or safety, but we stayed with a horse and buggy owner who assured us that he wanted to be our friend for the day. Finally, we made our way through the crowds to the horse and buggy stand. We picked a white horse to take us in to town.

But, that horse was only a lure to catch customers. As soon as we settled into the buggy, a dark-skinned Egyptian with a toothless smile came up and commanded us to get out and ride in another one drawn by a terribly skinny black horse. Our 'friend for the day' just shrugged his shoulders and handed us over to the toothless driver.

The driver introduced himself with a small bow, pointing one bony hand to his chest: "Me: Mohammed. Mohammed okay."

We explained in pidgin English where we wanted to go. "Mohammed: I Bettine... This Liz. We like see Mosque and Bazaar. But, we no millionaires. We crew on big boat."

Why did we speak in such stupid English in order to be better understood by Mohammed, I wonder to myself? I really don't know, but almost all English-speaking foreigners fall into this same routine no matter in what country they find themselves. I remember my husband asking a Japanese taxi driver to take him to the *QE2* at her dock in Okinawa. "El Porto," Peter said boldly in this international pidgin. He ended up at the airport twenty kilometers away.

Mohammed smiled showing just a few very yellow teeth. "I make good price. Cheap price: six dollar for one hour and I your guide." It sounded reasonable to us after all the bids at the dockside, some as high as fifty dollars. We accepted.

Settled on six dollars, Mohammed now rattled the reins of the dreadfully undernourished horse. Off we went in the little buggy. As soon as we were out in the crowded streets of Alexandria, Mohammed turned around to cajole us in a unique mixture of English, German, and Egyptian. We learned his life's story amid a stream of historical details concerning the passing landmarks.

"Here King Farouk morto kaput," he informed us. Liz and I looked at each other in amusement.

"What on earth does he mean?" Liz whispered. "It's like playing charades." After a bit of a discussion, we decided that this palace must have been where King Farouk died.

Mohammed never looked ahead at the horrendous traffic. We just hoped for the best; the little horse seemed to know its job.

Finally, after passing a delta stream of the Nile, we turned into the street with the big mosque. The horse and buggy parked, we all walked up to the enormous structure. At the entrance we pulled huge scarves from our bags. Women must cover their heads and shoulders to step on Muslim holy ground. Mohammed was our guardian, carefully arranging each scarf so only our eyes showed. It would have been disrespectful to reveal our bare feminine shoulders or to express a smile. My backpack bear was strapped to my shoulders. "Can he go in?" I asked. "Are bears allowed?" Mohammed pulled the scarf down over Bacpac so that I looked like Quasimoto. Bacpac was going in.

Inside, we peered up into the vast domed ceiling of the mosque, awed by the huge space. A few people were kneeling in one corner, casting suspicious looks at us. I quickly pulled my stole over my half-naked arms. Liz stooped a bit to keep her long skirt over her ankles. We knelt down and spent some twenty minutes in silence. It was very peaceful. Many have come here over the centuries to rest from their problems and the tensions of life.

Eventually, Mohammed became impatient and beckoned for us to leave. Around the corner stood a small side mosque. As soon as I saw it, I remembered that it was here on my last visit that I had played my Chinese flute in a secret chamber. Women are not usually allowed in this place, but they had made an exception for me.

As we approached the entrance, I recognized the same two Egyptian men from my last visit. They were the mullahs. They recognized Bacpac and within a few seconds they grabbed my arm in recognition. I was led again into the innermost chamber of the mosque, Liz wondering what in hell was happening. The mullahs smelled awful and their smiles were grotesque. I stumbled nervously along, hoping for the best. What would happen if they accosted me in this dark place? No one would come to my aid. But, my innermost self said, "It's all right," and Bacpac was there to protect me.

Inside the little room I saw the same huge sarcophagus which contained some bones of Mohammed (the religious leader Mohammed, of course, not our guide.) Just as it happened four years before, they pointed to it and smiled. I smiled back and said over and over: "Very beautiful... very beautiful." Then they pointed to the flute sticking out of my backpack bear. So, I slipped the backpack off my shoulders, took out my flute and started to play. The two mullahs began to sway to the rhythm, and then we all started dancing and laughing, our happy sounds resounding in this usually silent room.

They picked up Bacpac Bear and kissed him as they danced. There was so much joy in their faces. It suddenly hit me that we were having a celebration of souls. We were recognizing each other and experiencing that part which is so far beyond any particular religion—the spark, the spirit, and the essence within us all. It was a timeless moment.

I played a few more tunes. Then, suddenly we all smiled and it was over. They escorted me back to the entrance.

Liz jumped up: "What happened to you in there? I was really worried!" she screamed.

"Nothing," I answered grinning, "We just had a party."

"A party?" she shouted indignantly. "Why wasn't I invited?"

I hugged the two mullahs "Good-bye" as Liz gave me the strangest look that expressed both relief and indignation.

Mohammed seemed relieved, too. He was glad this part of our excursion was over. He was quite protective of us and he quickly ushered us back to the buggy with its ever-patient, skinny horse.

On our way back to the ship, Mohammed asked us about our lives. I took out some of my many photos to show him. They are a colorful variety of scenes from my childhood in Bavaria with my horses, the mountains, my parents and brothers, my travels to China including the kiss of the camel, and my wedding pictures.

Mohammed smiled broadly showing his two yellow teeth. I could not help thinking how much a dentist could have helped him. He certainly needed dentures, but a bath would have gone a long way to make him more acceptable in the Western world. He took out a small wallet to show us his pictures. They fell to the floor of the buggy. We quickly collected them up before they had a chance to blow away. Among them there was a recent snapshot of his two children and an older picture of his wife.

Mohammed looked sad and somber. "My woman... Morto kaput," he said. Tears welled up in his eyes.

I couldn't hold back my own tears. I let the sorrow flow. I could feel his pain and loneliness.

All of this happened while the little horse trotted through the crowded streets of Alexandria, with Mohammed all the time facing the back of the buggy. I looked at his dark face framed against the horse and the oncoming traffic chaos, appreciating this shared moment in time.

Finally, after two stops at "My brothers' stores," where we were expected to buy carpets, perfume or jewelry (naturally Mohammed would receive a pecuniary kick back), we reached the ship. Mohammed helped us out of the buggy and cleared his throat to make a speech.

"Mohammed lonely," he stated pointing to his heart. "Now Mohammed has friend," and he pointed to us.

I felt very moved. "Yes, we are your friends," I said, "And thank you for this wonderful day."

We paid him at the beginning of the trip, but he held out his hand for bachsheesh: "For my two children... very hungry," he pleaded.

We gave him another dollar bill and he was overjoyed. What a contrast of worlds: there are so many rich people on ships who complain if their appetizer is not perfect, and here we experienced the total poverty of Mohammed whose main worry was physical survival in each moment. Seven dollars was a lot of money to him, but meant far less to us than what we had learned and enjoyed of each other. Our experiences had awakened us to a mutual appreciation of the fleetness and piquant joys of life.

As I waved "Good-bye" to Mohammed and his skinny horse, I wondered when I would see him again. Where and when had I met him before? I don't think it was in this life.

The next day, I went in to Cairo. From Alexandria one has two choices—the slower road through the rich farmland of the Nile delta, or the faster direct road through the desert. I had taken the direct road before as tour busses usually favor this, but this time I took the delta road. My taxi driver was very attentive on the journey in stopping at appropriate places for me to experience an Egypt that has changed little since the Pharaohs. Ancient mud-built dovecotes washed in white lime stood in the rich fields of soil nurtured by centuries of the Nile floods. When I asked why there were so many dovecotes, he explained how important pigeons were in the rural Egyptian pre-wedding bachelor feast! Everywhere those fanned palms that I always associate with Cleopatra stood like sentinels as if they were the feathered fans behind the Pharaoh's throne. Ancient water wheels turned by water buffaloes or sick-looking mules fed irrigation streams. Others worked small flourmills or external-threshing stones such as had been used for four or five millennia. Women bent over in the fields of vegetables while men stood in groups discussing the affairs of the day. Boys fished from the riverbanks. Here, is the timeless Egypt of the Nile. But this fertile land only has width in this delta area. Further upstream it becomes a thin band that only follows the banks of the mighty river itself, a maximum width of no more than four miles.

Cairo in contrast to the peaceful beauty of the Nile Delta has to be one of the most polluted cities in the world. Dust and the fumes of poorly maintained motor cars lay heavily on the air. The people were aggressive and I really could not wait to leave. I visited the Cairo Museum—an incredible collection poorly lit and badly displayed. But, for me, as for most, the highlight had to be the fabulous Tutankamen exhibit. The boy king was assuredly buried with some of the greatest treasures of our world. But, my driver could not give me long; he was anxious to take me to the Sphinx and the Pyramids. I had been before and I feared the worst. The great pyramids of Giza are actually right on the very edge of the city where the pollution of Cairo meets the purer desert.

There are two common traps for tourists visiting Giza. One is the camel drovers, who eagerly await for their clientele to ride the relatively short distance from the camel lots up to the Great Pyramid of Cheops. At first they are all over the unsuspecting visitor promising all sorts of deals as they get you seated on their camel. Before you have time to adjust to the large ungainly saddle, the beast is pulled up to full height by the drover who smiles with a toothless grin similar to that of my friend Mohammed. The drover's name is probably Mohammed, too, as he will then explain as he pulls the camel along at a gentle pace. They are usually very ingratiating at this stage telling us how beautiful we look and encouraging us to have our photographs taken. It's a fairly safe bet that a tourist on the way to visit the pyramids is carrying a camera. He offers to take your picture to which you enthusiastically agree. But, as soon as this is accomplished, he demands payment—usually twenty dollars! From then on, unless you just pay up, violent arguments ensue and the drover begins to curse you and spit. This encourages the camel to spit, too! By the time you reach the Great Pyramid you can't wait to get away from the rude and rough man, but you can't, because he demands twenty dollars from you before he will make the camel kneel for you to dismount. Further arguments ensue, while a bevy of small children come up trying to sell you postcards.

Typical though this scenario may be, I was prepared from previous experience, and often when traveling alone and not with a tour bus, one is treated with rather more respect. My ride to the pyramids turned out to be rather pleasant and my drover was happy to receive ten dollars!

The second trap is the papyrus factory, which always seems to be beside a major tourist store where the unsuspecting visitor is herded in to be bribed by a cool Coca-Cola to make purchases of every conceivable item of modern junk. However, interesting papyri can be purchased at the factories, and on this occasion I made a purchase for my husband.

I was not prepared for a third trap. My driver wanted me to meet his family whom he informed me lived close by. They did, but it so happened that his wife ran a perfume shop. I don't use perfume, but as I sat in this part living room and part shop, his wife plied me with hot tea and sticky sweet cake. Meanwhile, my driver kept bringing out perfume bottles that all looked like they belonged in Aladdin's cave. He was so persistent that there was no way I could be driven back to Alexandria until I had made a purchase at an exorbitant price that offset the fairly good deal I had made for the taxi for the day! The smell of the perfumes made me feel nauseous, and in the end I paid him for a bottle just so that we could get out of there and drive on. Later, back on board my ship, I threw the bottle away.

I never have learned my lesson with the persistence of Egyptian camel drovers. I had enjoyed such a good relationship with camels in China that they continue to fascinate me. Besides, even in Egypt, it is not the camels, but the drovers that upset one. A new camel adventure waited for me the next time I was in Egypt when I was traveling with my husband on the *Royal Viking Sun*. We were making our way up the Red Sea toward Aqaba. We stopped at the new resort area of Sharem-al-Sheik, at the tip of the Sinai peninsula. I had booked a tour that had sounded incredible: a camel safari through the Sinai desert including lunch with Bedouin tribesmen in a nomadic tent. Peter went with me, along with about twenty-five passengers on tour. We were driven into the desert to a waiting herd of camels and were then each assigned to a beast, but also to a camel drover. On this occasion most of the camel drovers were children between the age of seven and sixteen. Our camel drover was a young, skinny-looking girl of about ten years with a sweet smile. So far so good. We mounted the kneeling camels, which then got up with lots of noise and groans and we took off into the desert.

The camels I had ridden both at the Pyramids in Egypt and also in China had always felt fairly comfortable to ride, but they were not safari camels! As soon as we started off swaying back and forth, I realized that this was to be different—a big challenge. Every time the camel took a step, the wooden pommels of this wretched, hard saddle poked into my stomach and then with the next step bruised my spine. That might have been bearable for ten minutes, however we were scheduled for a three-hour camel safari. Looking around at the others, I could easily see that they had the same problem, especially the more overweight riders. One man started to scream and already nobody looked as if they were enjoying the experience. I swung my legs up and sideways resting them on the camel's neck in the fashion that I had seen used by the Bedouin. The pain eased enough to allow me to appreciate the magic of the desert and the vastness of this mystical landscape. One could imagine Lawrence of Arabia suddenly appearing on the horizon and coming closer until it all disappeared into a mirage. It was very hot. My spine started to throb and my stomach hurt like hell. Mercilessly, the Egyptian girl marched on, at times yanking at the reins of the camel for no reason. We just had to endure the torture and hang in there.

Finally, after what seemed like an eternity (the relativity of time always amazes me), we came to our first rest stop. It was just out in the middle of nowhere, and all the camels came to a halt. With lots of groaning and moaning they knelt down again, and we could finally dismount and stretch our sore muscles. But there was no peace despite the greater ease.

The young drover girl stretched out her hand. "Bachsheesh!" she yelled with a screechy voice and her sweet smile transformed into a demanding harsh face.

We had already paid her at the beginning, so I said: "Later"

"No! Now!" she screamed.

I walked away, but she ran after me pulling on my shirt and took my hand and pointed at my wedding ring, an antique diamond ring, and a gift of love from Peter.

"Gimme, gimme!" she yelled.

"No!" I countered again. I was certainly not giving her my wedding ring! The girl went off in an angry huff to consult with her fellow drovers. Why was she so aggressive?

I calmed myself by playing my Tibetan flute for the camels. My camel looked up, gulped on the air and spat, but others showed more enthusiasm in their curiosity, and relieved passengers gathered around enjoying the break from their discomfort.

But, the break was not for long; the safari was ready to start again. We mounted our camels once more. Our child camel drover was angry. She had not gotten her way and she let us know it. She started yanking at my camel before we were settled, throwing me off my balance as I struggled to hold on to the pommel. She continued yanking at the poor beast causing it to stumble and every time that happened the saddle would cut right into my bruised spine and stomach. I closed my eyes and prayed that this would be over soon. I asked myself why I had created this torture? Was it to find out how much pain I could endure? Several of the passengers had dismounted and were now walking next to their camels falling to the rear of the train. No way would our angry girl let us down, however, she yanked harder on the camels and made them run. The pain was excruciating. All the time she was cursing me.

I felt myself getting angry now. I started to judge and curse that little devil that was making this trip so hard for us. 'What a spoiled brat,' I thought. And then, all of a sudden it hit me: I saw myself walking next to the camel and yanking the camel in impatient anger. I was seeing myself! I, myself, had many times acted out of anger, too, and yet always had resented and totally resisted that side of me. Yet, I often had experienced guilt feelings about my own outbursts of anger, especially when my mother died. I judged myself deeply for having been angry and impatient with her. I had not managed at this stage to really embrace, own and then let go of my anger. And here was the perfect mirror, right in front of my eyes in the middle of the Sinai desert on a hot camel safari that turned out to be an unexpected hardship. This little devil of a girl had pushed my buttons so much, so that I could finally see a quality that I had resented in myself. I decided that this was at least one very positive side effect of this safari and may be this could be some kind of a safari into the darker sides of my consciousness.

The sun was burning down on us. I started to think about Lawrence of Arabia again. How could he have stood that camel riding for so long? Our girl was still angry. She mumbled to herself, and hit the camel in her fury. But, rather than judge her I thought of my own childhood tantrums when I, too, had hit my pony that I loved so much. I smiled as I called down to her: "Please don't do that. Slow down. Don't hurt the camel." I am not sure if she really understood me, or whether she melted to my smile, but she stopped beating the camel in anger and mellowed down. By the time we reached the Bedouin tent for our desert luncheon, we had become quite good friends and she posed for many photographs. Everybody was so very grateful that we had finally arrived and could get off those camels. One could hear the sighs of relief, and many exclaimed: "Thank God that's over!" At this point I gave our drover girl her "bachsheesh" even though at times she had been such a devil. I am sure life in the desert is hard, but it is sad that there has to be so much aggression, and hostility. The lunch in the tent with the Bedouin turned out to be a welcome rest and even though the goat meat was tough, everything seemed great after the long camel ride. Fortunately, a minibus picked us up and brought us back to the ship. Once aboard, we could soothe our tortured backs and legs in a hot bath. But, the beauty of that desert scenery of Sinai will haunt me forever.

Since this experience, I have always enjoyed recommending to my audiences that if they ever go on a camel ride they should select one with two humps! Such were the camels in China and they are far more comfortable to ride than these one-humpers with those horrific saddles! But, then, not many places would be able offer you this choice: "How would you like your camel... Two humps or one?"

An overnight sailing up the Gulf of Aqaba brought us to the Jordanian port of the same name. We were still in the desert part of the world, but Aqaba is the sea's gateway to one of the desert's most spectacular ancient cities—Petra, which literally means the city of "The rocks." I had heard so much about this wonderful place from Peter who had used Petra as a major setting for sections of his trilogy of novels about Jesus and Mary Magdalene. I went with great anticipation to Petra although this time Peter had to remain in Aqaba. The two-hour bus ride brought us through rugged mountains and desert plains. Our official Jordanian guide talked nonstop about Biblical places associated with Abraham, Moses and others of those older guys who had walked and lived centuries ago. I tuned out with my "Walkman" wired in for sound and enjoyed piano preludes by Chopin which seemed to be perfect music for the mystical mood of the desert scenery and enabled me not to have to listen to all those Bible stories. I felt that the present moment was so much more powerful than all those references to a distant past. Finally, we came to the entrance of Petra.

Petra is a natural depression in the rocky desert that is fed by springs and inaccessible except through a long narrow winding track through

Writing a letter to
my French beau,
age 6 - 1955

Dressed as
Little Red
Riding Hood,
age 6 - 1955

Bonding with our
dog *Mucki* - 1955

On the horizon with *Svadi* my Icelandic pony - 1960

Show Jumping,
Bavaria - 1966

My childhood home in the snow, Bavaria

With my mother Ursula Clemen near Endorf - 1968

My father Wolfgang Clemen on Mount Parnassos, Greece

With my father in 1978

With horses in Iceland - 1992

A lifelong love for horses

A Camel's kiss, China - 1985

A Camel's breath, China - 1985

Riding *Hermitage*, a faithful friend in St. Petersburg, Russia

Cuddling a Koala, Australia - 1998

With my husband Peter Longley and a Koala, Australia - 1995

Playing for Kangaroos, Australia - 1995

Playing for a Goat at the Minnesota State Fair, Minneapolis - 1998

Playing for a Penguin, Tierra del Fuego, Chile - 1997

Penguins and the QE2, Falkland Islands - 1993

Playing a Contra Bass Flute

Playing the Bass Flute which I sometimes call 'my Hoover Vacuum Cleaner.'

With my European Guitar partner, Barbara Polasek

After recording with members of the Prague Radio Chamber Orchestra
Jan Peruska - violist and Miloslav Hrdlik - double bass - 1989

With World Renowned Concert Pianist Lorin Hollander - 1993

With my American Guitar partner, Richard Patterson in Alaska

With my Celtic Harpist partner, Kim Robertson

With Russian Balalaika Virtuoso and Conductor Emanuil (Misha)
Sheynkman

With Russian Concert Pianist Nana Mukhadze and 'Bacpac'

Playing on the
Great Wall of
China - 1985

Playing from a Two Hump Camel, China - 1985

Teaching Chinese children, Beijing, China - 1985

With Chinese
composer
Tan Mi Zi,
Shanghai,
China - 1985

'Flute Talk,' China - 1985

With Flautists from the Beijing Symphony, China - 1985

In Concert with the Beijing String Quartet - 1985

With Prof. Lin Keh-Ming announcing my Concert, Beijing, China -
1985

Satisfying
Chinese
Customs - 1985

With my dog *Lara*
in Brazil - 1979

'Young Audiences.'

With a young friend on board the Royal Viking Sun - 1997

Intense response on board the Royal Odyssey - 1996

Riding out in Iceland - 1992

Donkeys in Jordan - 1996

Petra Portrait, Jordan - 1996

Playing for Jordanian youths, Petra - 1996

Tai Chi on the beach, New Zealand - 1994

With friends from Africa - 1992

With famed Photographer Courtney Milne performing a multi-media Concert with The Saskatoon Symphony in Canada - 1997

At the Ba'Hai Temple, Haifa, Israel - 1994

A 20th Century encounter with 'The Caretaker' of the Garden of Gethsemane, Jerusalem, Israel - 1994

With Nuns from the Presentation Convent, Cashel, Co. Tipperary, Ireland - 1998

Surrounded by Sheep, Co. Tipperary, Ireland - 1998

In the Captain's Quarters on board the QE2 - 1997
From Left to Right: Commodore John Burton-Hall, Actress Jenny
Agutter, Author Dick Francis, Lady Mills, TV Presenter Barry
Norman, Myself, Actor Sir John Mills, Rosemary Burton-Hall and
part of her charity collection of 'Care Bears.'

With my husband Peter Longley and Captain Robin Woodall on
board the QE2 - 1994

Cruising in
Alaska - 1989

A Visit to the Jean-Michel
Cousteau Resort,
Savusavu, Fiji - 1996

On Our Wedding Day, June 19th, 1993

On Our Wedding Day, June 19th, 1993

With Peter on our Honeymoon canoeing in the Okefenokee Swamp,
Georgia - 1993

the rocks. It was the capital of the Nabataeans at the time of Jesus, and because of the enormous wealth that it had accumulated as a crossroads of desert trade, it was watched eagerly by the rising power of Rome. Eventually, it was absorbed into the Roman Empire in the time of Emperor Hadrian during the early Second Century AD. The ruins of both the Nabatean and Roman civilizations can be found preserved in this desert wonder, whose crowning glory is not so much in her historical significance as in the magnificent color of her rocks.

One can still ride up to this entrance on fiery Arabian horses. I was lucky enough to get a spirited white beast, which even galloped. My backpack holding my flutes and other sundry items, rattled as it jumped up and down, and I felt the exhilaration I had always felt when speeding on horseback. But, at the entrance I had to dismount. From hereon in one has to walk or be driven in by chariot. The path into the steep canyon is amazing! As I walked between these high, pink-colored canyon walls that rise up naturally and above which only glimpses of the blue sky and overhanging trees can be seen, I felt the mystique. Then, after about ten minutes, all of a sudden the narrow entranceway opens onto one of the most incredible buildings in the world... the Treasury Building! My heart stood still—what a sight! This building, like most the great Nabatean tombs of Petra was carved out of the solid rock... this beautiful naturally rose-colored stone. Its face was intricately decorated with Nabatean scrolls intermingling with Greek classic images. Our guide explained that the cliff building was carved out of the face exactly during the years that Jesus walked the Earth.

It was fairly early in the morning. Not too many tourists were about yet, so I ran into the Treasury Building. Inside, I took out my Tibetan flute and started to play—the echo was exquisite! The notes just hung on the air before bouncing back from the walls!

Further down, following the canyon road, which had now widened out, I ran into another camel! This one was hunched up all by itself. I gave it a short concert on another bamboo flute. As soon as I started to play, the camel closed its eyes, and went into some kind of a trance, or at least that is what it looked like to me. Then, some people came by. They could not believe the expression on this camel's face, and then to the surprise of us all, the beast started to sway with its head to the rhythm of the music. I felt again that strange bond and attraction to camels that I had experienced in China, even though I was still hurting from the desert ordeal of the safari the day before.

Passing an impressive theater, its tiers of seats set into the cliff face, I was reminded of an English pianist whom I had met on board the *QE2*. He had played a concert here and they had lowered his piano into the theater by helicopter. Of course, this concert in Petra was a good promotion, but I could not help also sensing the drama of such an event surrounded as I now was by such colorful cliffs and incredible carved tombs. I climbed up many steps beyond the theater to one of these vast Nabatean tomb caves that looked out over Petra from its high rock walls. I hoped that there would not be too many people inside and therefore I might be able to play again and enjoy the echo. There were just a few other entertainers from the ship accompanying me into that cave and I asked them if they would mind if I played. They had nothing against it and soon the cave was filled with sounds. As I started to play, two of the entertainers started to chant and sing. I discovered that they had embraced Buddhism and were used to chanting. Now, they shared these hauntingly beautiful sounds with me. I chanted, too. While they were doing their Buddhist chant, I chanted "Hu," the sacred name for God, and others then joined in the hum. Time stood still. The power of the sound engulfed us. Many other people appeared from nowhere. They stood there in amazement. We kept going for some time and then, as naturally as this sound feast had started, it faded, with the last notes hanging in the space like jewels suspended in time.

We were all somewhat speechless. The people applauded and told us that they had heard this sound coming out of the cave from far away and that they were just drawn to it. It was a very precious moment, and I felt on a natural high. I could feel the presence of all the history that had happened here and yet this moment was the most powerful one.

After a brief exploration of the Roman city, it was time to head back to the entrance. On my way I ran into a group of about fifteen teenagers from Jordan, who were English students. I stopped and chatted with them for quite some time. They were so interested and eager to learn, and very grateful and fun to be with. We took photos and exchanged addresses and I again felt this great inter-connection and love that comes from that part within us that is universally of the same essence, be it in camels, donkeys, people or the stars of our universe.

Sometimes now, I travel back to Petra in my imagination and enter that rock tomb cave and listen to the sounds within. It is a magical place and its mystique has inspired many to reach inside themselves, both in the past and now.

When we came to Haifa, Israel, several days later, it was time for me to get off the ship. I had been touring now for two and a half months straight and my contract with this ship ended here. Peter had to fly straight home from Telaviv, but I had reserved several days here to share with my guitarist accompanist and friend from Germany, Barbara. It was my first visit to Israel. Barbara had suggested that we stay at the Mount Zion monastery in Jerusalem, and when I first heard about this plan I imagined a real monastic scenario with bunk beds and lots of monks, so I said to her: "The last thing I want to do is to sleep on the floor with a bunch of monks!"

"But Bettine, that is not at all how it will be," she countered, "We will have our own room and meals, too! But don't let them know that you are not Catholic!"

"Don't worry," I assured her, "I can behave for a couple of days!"

'I am not even Christian,' I thought. 'But, why should that really matter?'

I had never been able to relate very much to the human tendency to separate all of us according to our religious or cultural labels, nor to the strange habit of humans fighting over who has the better or the older or even the "only name" for different interpretations of the same source.

When we finally reached Jerusalem, I was very moved by the beauty of this historic city. The monastery turned out to be a blessing! The monks were extremely hospitable and friendly and showed us to our own simple, but comfortable room. We were to share the meals with them and could also attend their services of Vespers and the Mass if we wished. Barbara is a strict Roman Catholic and so we did. I must say that although the services didn't mean much to me, I loved the chanting and we felt very welcome and at home.

From the Monastery we went out and explored the sights of Jerusalem including Gethsemane and Golgatha. I constantly thought of my husband. Peter had just completed *The Magdala Trilogy*. It was, after all, his discussion of these books that had so fascinated me on that night when we had first really talked to each other on board the *QE2*. Now, here I was myself in the very place where a lot of the key events took place.

When I entered the garden of Gethsemane on the slopes of the Mount of Olives, I felt like sitting alone in silence for a while. Barbara wandered off on her own as I sat on a large rock overlooking Jerusalem. Here it was that supposedly Jesus asked if "this cup could be taken from me?" I started to contemplate on the question. How much of this really was as it is described in the Bible? Maybe it could have also been quite different. I remembered so well that Maria of Magdala played an important part in Peter's interpretation of the story and that she and Jesus, or Joshua in Peter's novels had actually been very close. Eventually, they had become lovers here in this very garden of Gethsemane. Here, in Peter's novel, Maria had conceived Jesus' son just a few days before the crucifixion. Sadly, Jesus never knew this. As my thoughts dwelt on this possible scenario here in this ancient garden and the great spiritual love on all levels that might have been there between Joshua and Maria, I realized that I was possibly creating my own memory of the past, and that the past does not really exist until we create a memory of it in the present.

I was jerked out of my emotional pondering by the voice of a man: "You enjoy the view?" I looked around and saw a small, but hefty-looking man, standing behind me. He had a broad and warm smile and his white teeth were in strong contrast to his brown sunburned, wrinkled face.

"Yes it is very special here for me!" I answered.

"I am the gardener," the man explained, and for a moment I felt jolted back to the First Century AD, despite the fact that I had just questioned the existence of linear time. In an instant I saw the familiar scene: Maria of Magdala after the crucifixion arriving as the first one at Jesus' tomb and realizing that the body of her beloved was not there. She was afraid, and then she met the gardener and recognized in him a great kindness. He listened to her and comforted her. He showed divine love and compassion. But, the significant thing was that she recognized the "Christ consciousness" in him. She was transformed by that recognition and it did not matter to me any more whether he really was the risen "Christ" as the Bible says, or just the gardener, because her soul awoke in that moment to the greater awareness that we all can be as "Christ," an anointed one.

The gardener now opened his hand and showed me a coin that he wanted to give me. It was a beautiful old coin with the star of David on one side. I got up and thanked him. I was not quite sure in which time this took place, but when I shook his solid hands and thanked him looking him in the eye, I realized that it was irrelevant whether this was in a past life or happening right now. I had felt and witnessed the exchange of divine love with the gardener, just like Mary Magdalene had two thousand years ago. This phrase went through my head: "Soul is eternal and lives only in the present moment." Now, looking into the sparkling eyes of a stranger... this gardener, I realized that I was also looking at myself as soul and that we can all awaken in each other.

It was time to find Barbara. We wanted to visit the Church of Mary Magdalene, with its Russian-style onion shaped domes. We attended a service there. There were only nuns and one priest. It was very serious and very dark. I felt no joy. The nuns all looked so sad and were constantly asking for forgiveness and to be saved by Jesus. The priest came out of a secret door several times and kissed the Bible and did all kind of rituals that I didn't understand. The whole atmosphere was sinister and suppressive—there was no joy! I felt that the real essence of the divine message had happened for me in my exchange with the gardener in the mystique of Gethsemane. Nothing happened for me in this dark and depressing church. On our way out, we passed the Mother Superior and I thanked her for allowing us to attend. I also mentioned that I was very fond of Mary Magdalene. The little old nun in her black habit suddenly came alive: "Oh yes! Mary Magdalene!" she exclaimed. "She was possessed by seven devils and Jesus had to drive them out of her! He saved her! She was a big sinner!" I cast my eyes down and bit my tongue. I wanted to say something to her, but I decided not to. I just thought it. 'It is also quite possible that Mary Magdalene helped Jesus and that she was a very spiritual woman, who healed with her love and compassion.' Who knows—it is just as possible, probably more so!

The total condemnation and denial of love's expression in a physical and sensual way by the Church has caused millions to lead totally unhappy and suppressed lives and is to me one of the most unfortunate misunderstandings, not only of Christianity, but of many religions. It has cut people off from their life force and has forced them into suppression, guilt feelings and often perversions. Our most natural talents and powers have been made "of the devil," and that has psychologically screwed up mankind. And even if Mary Magdalene were a prostitute, as many seem to believe, why would that be any cause for us to judge her negatively? She probably helped many through her love. As I stood before the Mother Superior, I considered it best to keep quiet and leave.

The next day Barbara and I gave two concerts. The first was for our dear Benedictine monks at Mount Zion and the other was for the two hundred-year celebration of the Austrian archdiocese's connection with Jerusalem. The Archbishop of Austria was present and we had a wonderful time there. Our concert was to be at a reception followed by a huge dinner. But before all that, we had to attend Mass in the small church. This was all in the "old city" part of Jerusalem, and the evening coincided with the end of the Moslem holy period of Ramadam. The windows of the chapel were open and while we were singing Latin Christian hymns in the church, one could hear the sounds of Moslem chants coming through the window. What a strange moment! Sounds and music of these different religions being expressed in a quest for some truth, but proclaiming that they have the only truth. We are all of the same essence as spiritual beings but unfortunately as human beings we often forget our real nature. Here in Jerusalem it became even more evident to me how absurd are the wars and animosities made in God's name.

The Austrian Archbishop turned out to be a very jolly man and I got to sit next to him at dinner. We got along fantastically well. I was wearing a red Punjabi from India, which fascinated him. He looked me up and down and said: "You are wearing the exact right dress for being an Archbishop; the only thing missing is the red cap!"

I laughed and answered: "Well, maybe there is still some hope for me!"

There are wonderful people in all religions and the problems only start when they think that they have the only solution. We ate and celebrated until late into the night. Then, about one in the morning we walked home through the "old city" escorted by our friends from the Mount Zion monastery, Brother Mattheus and Brother Marcus. Mattheus was carrying my bass flute and Marcus carried Barbara's guitar case. The Ramadam celebrations had quieted down. One could only hear the sound of our steps on the hard cobblestones that looked as if they were from the same time when Jesus had walked these roads. I felt a shiver going through my blood. We paused for a moment of eternal quietness overlooking the roofs of Jerusalem. Mattheus started to sing. Marcus, Barbara and I joined in. It was a simple love song to God—to us as divine beings. It will ring in my soul forever.

In the Mediterranean there are such overlays of history and invariably these are linked to the spread of Christianity. One time I cruised through the Mediterranean with Kim, my Celtic harpist friend. We were supposed to board a ship in Madeira, Portugal. A secretary with little geographic knowledge at head office wanted to send us there by train from Lisbon! There was a delay in the time it took them to discover that Madeira is an island out in the middle of the Atlantic! It was then too late for us to join our ship in Madeira and they had to fly us to Malaga, Spain, the ship's next port of call.

I'd never been to Spain before so the change in plan afforded the opportunity to explore. But, first we had to get from the airport to the ship with Kim's harp. Many taxi drivers accosted us in rapid Spanish as we emerged from the airport. Kim tried her French and I my Portuguese, neither of which they understood. Finally, we put Kim's harp on top of a taxi and set off at great speed through the crowded streets. We worried about the harp at every twisting curve.

We reached the ship in one piece and successfully unloaded the harp in time to spend much of the day exploring this southern tourist city which is Spain's gateway to Andalusia. We then embarked on our month long cruise of the Mediterranean and Northern Europe stopping in a different port each day. We would play our concerts in the evenings on board and arrive at a major city or interesting venue to explore by day. Our first stop was Barcelona.

It was high season and Barcelona was very crowded. On tour, Kim and I found that humming a familiar sound or song helped us cope with our unaccustomed rehearsal schedules and the often-frustrating nature of these hectic cities. From Citavecchia in Italy we took a train into Rome. There, we met our cellist-friend, Anthea, who showed us the highlights of the Coliseum, St. Peter's basilica, and the Vatican.

We hummed to ourselves in St. Peter's and among the vast crowds in the square outside. This calmed us amid the bustle. One could really feel the power of the Roman Catholic Church here, but in the basilica I couldn't help but be reminded of my experience in Jerusalem at the church of Mary Magdalene above Gethsemane. There was something oppressive and heavy about the interior. We took a bus through the city and I thought about how much more nature evoked spirituality in me than most churches and sacred buildings. My thoughts seemed in such contrast to the crowds of pilgrims thronging St. Peter's Plaza. Thoughts seem to evoke their own reality. As we stood being jostled in the crowded bus, an older man began to speak to me in English. He, too, was interested in spirituality and philosophy, which transformed the ride into something very uplifting. In contrast when Kim and Anthea got off the bus they complained that they had been pinched and pressed by some of the Italian men in the crowd.

On the bus journey back we got chatting with a group of nuns. The very back seats of the bus became available to us—such is the power of the Church! The nuns smiled sweetly as men who had occupied those seats made way for them. The nuns asked us how we were enjoying Rome and then offered to teach us how to say the rosary. We politely declined and began to talk to them about their work in the Vatican. It was fascinating, not only did they teach and live their religious life of prayer, but also they were the cleaners and housekeepers in this male-dominated celibate bastion. We parted with joy and friendship.

From Rome, we went to Genoa, where we had a special encounter. Kim and I went exploring with a comedian and juggler from the ship. After dinner, we wandered around again. The juggler found a little side street that led to a secret garden. When we went in we found a very beautiful, quiet old church. Here was the aura of quiet inner peace that I remembered in the Egyptian mosque. A priest, clad in a long robe, approached and spoke to us in flawless French. We had apparently come across a small Genoese monastery. The Genoese priest warmed to us and took us on a tour of the buildings. He showed us into a lovely side chapel with magnificent acoustics. Kim and I sang a chant of Ave *Maria*. Exquisite sounds hung on the air.

When we said "So long" to the priest, it was as if we had just spent an hour with an old, old friend, like Mohammed in Alexandria.

The next day, we wanted to find a shoe store in Genoa. We asked a passerby for advice, and he ended up walking with us for about fifteen minutes until we came to the doorway of an appropriate shop. Genoa was an extraordinarily friendly town. 'It is amazing how much goodness and kindness one can find in this troubled world,' I mused. 'All my traveling seems to reveal this more and more. It is a far cry from the TV screen news at home. One can find the essential goodness in soul.'

I wondered, however, if true spirituality could be found in churches and mosques. Peace... yes, but true spirituality... I wondered. Perhaps it lies in the little kindnesses of each day. Maybe that is a better way to experience God. I have visited mosques, churches and temples of Muslims, Christians, Hindus, Buddhists and Jews, yet all I remember are the eyes of the individual souls who welcomed me, as they shared a part of their hum drum lives with me... their heartfelt gestures represent to me what is truly divine... unconditional love.

## Chapter Eleven

# The Emerald Isle

E ver since I first visited Ireland as a teenager, this green island has always evoked a strange feeling of being home for me. It is a feeling of connectedness with the mystical and earthy qualities of the land, the uniqueness of its people, the intoxicating fresh air, the donkeys, horses and sheep everywhere and the magnificent beauty of its landscapes. I take every opportunity to go back there and share my love for Ireland with my husband, Peter, who lived in Southern Ireland for sixteen years when he was the estate manager of a castle in county Tipperary.

The rain is a constant companion in Ireland. On my most recent tour I was driving toward Tipperary for a concert date, trying to stay on the left-hand side of the road, and many images from my past visits came into my mind. The first time I came was with my mother in order to buy Connemara ponies at Clifden horse fair. Then, there was the memorable trip alone to Ireland when I was nineteen. I had been in love with my high school music teacher. He was the first man I could really open my heart to after my accident. I thought that I loved him so much that I even wanted to marry him. But, then he married another woman and I was heart broken. I traveled to Ireland by myself to heal my heart. It rained every day of those four weeks, but the Irish cheerfully assured me: "It has been fine six months ago!" and, therefore, there was a very good chance that it might be fine again, at least at some time. On my long walks in the rain around Dingle Bay, I discovered that they were filming a major epic called *Ryan's Daughter*, and I even met some of the cast and film crew. The special effects man (the one responsible for creating the rain and storm scenes, although I really don't think they needed any more rain) took me up to the reconstructed film set village in the hills above Dingle. Life started to flow again. My sadness washed away with all that rain and slowly and gently my heart opened again and I felt better. Little did I know that at the same time, my husband Peter Longley was a young man living in County Tipperary as an estate manager and that his employers had invited the principal cast members of *Ryan's Daughter* to their castle. It took another twenty-five years for us to meet. The time was not right yet.

As I drove out into the Irish countryside on this tour, now almost thirty years later, I took in the "nice soft day" as the Irish call these rainy days, and felt that strange intoxicating feeling again of being back in my beloved Ireland. I was scheduled to perform my concert in Cashel, but I had the day to myself. I had enough time to visit Glenstal Abbey near Limerick, a monastery of timeless and stunning beauty situated in a huge estate of gardens. It is also known as the abbey of the "singing monks." The Benedictine monks who live there practice their chanting about four times a day. I was hoping to hear them on my arrival at Glenstal. I reflected on the enormous influence that Celtic mysticism has had on our world.

On arrival, I was taken to see the Abbott, who was working in the garden weeding the flowers. He was a very gentle and bright man, who immediately invited me for tea, and then showed me around the abbey. Apart from the monastic house, the abbey is also home to about 200 students who go through high school here. The abbey is surrounded by huge gardens, one of them being a biblical garden, which was shown to me by another "brother" with great pride. "We have all those herbs here that are mentioned in the Bible, and also lots of vegetables and salad. We are almost totally self sufficient here," Brother Christopher explained.

"Will you be singing soon? " I asked.

"Yes we have a Vespers Service at 6 p.m. Can you stay?"

"I would simply love to," I answered.

The huge abbey church was almost empty except for about 10 to 15 visitors. Then, the monks came in. Quietly, they took their places. When they started to sing, the sound filled the church; it rose to the ceiling and circled around inspiring me and I felt a warm and uplifting energy enter my being. How real the power of sound can be! Every cell of my body soaked up the vibration and I felt the pure nourishing energy of the chants. I could truly appreciate the monks and what they had to offer. The sounds went beyond any differences in religion or philosophy and united us all in the realm of pure energy, where belief systems and dogmas cease to exist. It does not matter what one calls this divine energy. All that matters is that one feels it, experiences it and that it can transform us and ignite the awareness in us of our universal divinity.

Completely replenished and renewed, I stepped out into the sunlight and headed back to my car. I thanked the monks. They had extended so much hospitality to me and I felt deeply grateful for their kindness. We exchanged gifts: CDs and books. I looked back up at the abbey while I drove down through the gardens and saw Brother Christopher wave "Goodbye."

My concert was to be the next evening in the beautiful Cashel Cathedral. The funds were to go to the Nagle Home in Cashel, a home for disabilitated and mongoloid people suffering from dowsyndrome disease. I had played in this cathedral several times and looked forward to the great acoustics and ambiance again. But, this time something very special was about to happen. It had been arranged for me to also play a smaller concert at the Nagle Centre for the people there, and I also showed them some of my slides of animals from around the world. Two of the downsyndrome girls had been the artists for the poster for my concert. They had portrayed me in an almost Piccasso-like way, with the eyebrows being below the eye and the flute coming out of my mouth like a straw. I really loved those paintings and in my concert introduced and thanked the two artists. They beamed with pride. There were about forty patients at the Centre and they were extremely expressive and loving. They did not have any barriers or shyness demonstrating their love and joy completely naturally and spontaneously. They felt so much. During the concert they expressed with sounds and "Aahs" and "Oohs" how much they liked it and were so present and grateful. I tried a little experiment. I showed them all the different flutes.

"What do I have to do in order to get a sound out of one of those flutes?" I asked just as I do with 'Young Audiences' in American schools. Just like in my school programs, they shouted back: "Blow into them!" "Push the buttons!"

No sound came out of the flute. "What is wrong? What happened?" I asked.

Then, from the back row the answer came: "Batteries are low!" There was lots of laughter. The room was bursting with energy and joy.

'Why do we call these people disabilitated,' I thought, 'when they can teach us how to feel more and how to be more loving?'

After the concert, the warden of the Nagle Centre, a bright young man, invited me for lunch with all those attending the Centre. He explained that they were also running a deli in the town where people love to come. The deli is entirely run by the downsyndrome members of the Centre. The people come not only for the delicious sandwiches, but also for the experience of the very kind and innocently loving treatment they get from these people that we tend to call "disabilitated" and who are often treated as outsiders in our society. What a wonderful way to integrate them and to diminish or eliminate that separation. They also showed me their workshop, in which they made their arts and crafts. I expressed my admiration for their paintings and creations with enthusiasm and they responded with such genuine joy and natural pride, which is so seldom found among the so-called normal people. Their smiles were beaming and really came from their hearts. Many hugs were exchanged. I felt that here at the Nagle Centre real love was alive and well and that these people were bringing their gifts with open hearts to the world, sharing without compromise.

In the afternoon, I went back to my hosts to rest before the evening concert. I was staying this time with an Anglo-Irish family at a Regency house of the now somewhat reduced landed gentry, who were running a sheep farm. Fifteen hundred sheep surrounded the house creating both visual impressions along with their unique sounds and smells.

That evening, Cashel Cathedral filled up with several hundred people. I knew many of them from the past. While I was playing my first number called "Marble Halls," I noted that Denis Heffernan, the very special bartender of the Cashel Palace Hotel had also come to the concert together with his mother. Denis is such a unique character. He has been at the Palace for over thirty-five years and is famous for his unmatched humor and for singing songs like *Danny Boy* in the Bar. Later in the concert that evening I actually played *The Londonderry Air,* which is the instrumental original for *Danny Boy.* My arrangement is with string orchestra and flute. As I knew Dennis was there, I told the audience: "If you really want to hear one of the very best renditions of this air as a song, you should go to the bar of the Cashel Palace Hotel and have Dennis Heffernan sing it for you. You will never forget the rendering. Dennis is here tonight and I want to thank him for inspiring me and for teaching me the few phrases in Gaelic that I mentioned to you at the beginning of this concert. Dennis, thank you!" With that, Dennis got up from his seat and took a little bow. For this he received a huge cheer and a round of applause from the audience. Almost everybody in the cathedral knew him.

Dennis is very proud of the many interesting characters he has served over the years. He has many of their names painted up on the walls of his basement bar. I was somewhat flattered when he suggested that my name as a solo flautist should be added to join the likes of famous racehorse trainers such as Vincent O'Brien, jockeys of the standing of Lester Piggott and one time Olympic Games Chairman Lord Kilanin. He revealed, however, that one of the Palace's most notable visitors' names was not inscribed upon the wall. Apparently, and my husband corroborates in this as he was dining in the Palace that night, the notorious train robber Ronald Biggs, who ended up living in freedom in Rio de Janeiro, passed through Cashel while on the run. He stopped at Dennis' Bar for a drink.

"The Bar never emptied so fast," Dennis revealed. "A note was passed among the customers saying 'Biggs is here.' They all ran out like flies leaving me alone with one of the world's most wanted men. Of course, it has never been proved that the man was Biggs, but to be sure he had the splittin' image of your man."

The Cashel Palace is a wonderful old Queen Anne mansion in the heart of town with gardens leading up to the famed and illuminated 'Rock of Cashel,' one-time home of Brian Boru and the Kings of Munster. Today, this impressive ruin comprised of both castle and cathedral is floodlit at night by courtesy of the Guinness Foundation. Dennis is always proud to reveal the Palace's original connection with the Guinness family.

"You see, this great house was once the Palace of the Archbishops of Cashel. In them days, Archbishop Price had a butler who experimented with some hops growing here in the garden. The butler's name was Arthur Guinness. Them hops growing right here were what started the great brewery up in Dublin. You see to be sure this is a famous old house."

Dennis is right. Actually to this day, hop vines are preserved on either side of the steps going down from the Palace Drawing Room out into the gardens.

But, the Palace has had many different owners since it became a luxury hotel. In their wisdom, this succession of owners has retained the services of Dennis Heffernan. For many years, Dennis served with another unforgettable character—Festus.

Sadly, Festus has now passed away, but he lives on in legend at the Cashel Palace. Never has the world known a worse waiter. According to Dennis and others to whom I have spoken including my husband Peter, Festus could have been the archetype for *Fawlty Towers*. But, he was so bad, that he became an asset. People drove miles after race meetings to dine at the Cashel Palace just to experience 'Festus.' His bow tie was invariably adrift and his dinner jacket soiled with soup. On one occasion my husband witnessed Festus serve vegetables to a guest who had no plate. The vegetables were neatly piled up on the tablecloth! Another time he had a customer complain about the soup several times. Festus got so fed up with the customer that he finally yelled at the complainer: "You either eat that soup now or you leave our restaurant!" The shocked gentleman fearfully obliged and gobbled down the soup as fast as he could. Nobody ever got angry with Festus —they just laughed.

The Irish sense of humor is one of a kind. It is unique and can only be experienced. The Irish look at life from a somewhat different angle. I remember once getting lost in the Wicklow Mountains south of Dublin. Desperately looking for help, I finally spotted an Irishman standing beside the narrow road with his sheepdog. "How on earth can I get back to Dublin?" I asked.

After a pregnant pause, the man said in an Irish accent that I could not begin to imitate: "First of all young lady, I wouldn't start from here!"

What delightful logic!

In Ireland I saw some of the most unusual and the funniest of street signs. I remember driving through a small village in Southern Ireland and there was this huge sign in front of a restaurant:

*Special Offer! Buy Three Pizzas for the price of Four and get the Fifth one Free!*

It took me a moment to digest this, but then I saw that people were actually lining up!

Another sign in a different village read:

*Ears pierced while you wait!*

Now think about that for a moment! I wanted to go in to the shop and say: "Can I leave my ears and go to dinner and then pick them up later?"

And then, one of my very favorites which I saw near Athlone:

*Antiques! Old and New!*

In the west of Ireland one time, I passed a strawberry stand beside the road. In Ireland the little baskets that the strawberries are packed in are called punnets. Each punnet usually holds about fifteen to twenty strawberries. The sign at the roadside failed to mention the word punnet, however. It read:

*One Strawberry Two Pounds—Two Strawberries Three Pounds Fifty.*

These had to be the most expensive strawberries in the world!

After the concert in Cashel, the Nagle Centre had prepared a huge warm meal in their kitchen to which they invited about twenty guests. We talked and celebrated until late that night. I went home to the sheep farm with my hosts, filled with genuine joy over the happiness that these people were creating and with great appreciation of them for letting me share with them. But in contrast, that night I could not sleep for a long time.

My thoughts were with some young boys, who had been killed in a recent terrorist bombing in Northern Ireland and to whom I had dedicated the last selection of my Cashel Cathedral Concert. What a sad contrast—the total insanity of the intense violence in the happenings in the North and the tremendous gift of love that those inflicted with downsyndrome had shared with me at the Nagle Centre – the very people we tend to label as "Insane" or "Disabilitated."

Somehow, I hoped and felt that what each and every individual feels and expresses does make a difference. We are all interconnected, we are all part of the one, and everyone's individual gift of love helps the whole planet, as small and as insignificant as it might seem in the moment. Every thought and every feeling manifests and effects the whole! If we only knew how really powerful we are! When I finally closed my eyes that night, I saw the beaming and loving faces of the downsyndrome children in my inner vision. They were giving me strength.

For over thirty years the difficulties of political opinion over Northern Ireland's future have fueled violence and so many innocent people have suffered or been killed like those young boys to whom I dedicated my music. This violence, although limited to a small geographic area, has been world news, and a generation in Northern Ireland has grown up with associated prejudices fueled by bitterness and futile hostility.

I was booked recently on a flight from Minneapolis to London. Some forty children in *The Irish Children's Program* were also on board. This is a program whereby children from all religious and cultural backgrounds in Northern Ireland spend a month or more as summer guests in American families. Minneapolis has always been in the forefront of this program that has been working with children from Northern Ireland for about ten years. The idea is that within the American experience these children find that their friendships take them beyond any division of race, class or religion. I felt my heart open, as I watched the emotional scenes as these happy Irish children said "Goodbye" to their hosts at the Minneapolis/St. Paul Airport. I could feel how the love and kinship expressed could become the bridge that can ultimately transform rigid prejudices and thought patterns. These children could be the future hope for that troubled Province. They had opened their ears and hearts to love and that inner love will win in the end uniting the beauty of the Emerald Isle with the beauty of its people.

# Chapter Twelve

# *Nordic Light*

Often, I have summer land concerts in Europe during July and August and this also gives me the opportunity to accept further concert work on cruise vessels in Scandinavia. Prestigious ships are always sailing in the Norwegian fjords and up to the North Cape in Norway's "Land of the Midnight Sun."

I have been lucky on many of my journeys up and down this spectacular coast. I have witnessed many marvelous vistas of this mystical country. It can be 2:30 a.m. and the decks of the ship will still be crowded with passengers drinking in the magic of nights when the sun never sets. Even if it is cloudy, the rays of the midnight sun peek through the gaps filtering down to a sea that reflects their golden light. Drama unfolds as we pass snow-capped peaks. Sometimes, I have sailed beyond the North Cape up to the snow-covered mountains of Spitzbergen and then beyond to the polar ice cap within four hundred miles of the North Pole. Here, one can listen to the sound of silence—almost the purest music of all, creating a state of healing bliss. One becomes oblivious of the actual sounds of the talking ice flows jostling against one another and cracking up in the softening of the long summer day that lasts from Spring to Fall—the stillness of the pure air takes over leading one into a contemplative state. Here, is only the ice and the widest of skies.

Such silence is a fullness, a depth, a wealth, and a source for strength. Silence is an attitude, a willingness to be relaxed and open to life. You can learn many things from this. When you go within, into the silence of inner peace, it is rejuvenating. It is a path of purification. If you practice, you can leave the path of noise at will and pass through a door into your own healing temple. Wise people make a daily habit of focusing on this inner quiet where all truth, light, and healing sound arises. Any method or way of getting beyond the surface of life can lead to your inner temple. This is the place where we encounter the infinite awareness, that essence we really are. Contact with this aspect of our being brings unbounded internal peace, bliss and freedom. I have found that for me most inner growth comes out of such experiences of silence and the deliberate use of directing my attention.

Silence, however has become very rare today. About a hundred years ago, my grandfather Paul Clemen, who was a well-known German art historian, described in his journal how he walked from Bonn to Rome. Being an artist he decided to do this walk out of a sense of adventure. It took him five to six months to make the journey. He wrote of the stillness, which he experienced crossing the Alps and how it contrasted with the incredible noise of the Italian cities. I wonder what he would have said about our cities and towns today. He later wrote a poetic book, *Praise to the Silence*, in which he shared his insights into the value of silence. I was born one year after he died and even though I had not known him, I felt close to him because of his love for the inner space of silence.

A German poet, Bertram, said, "If you want to know who you are, and where you belong, try to be silent. Out of the bath of silence alone comes the word of creation."

So it is when you encounter the sound of silence. Standing at a ship's rail and looking into that Northern ice field that makes up the polar cap, I have sensed this sound of silence... I have found my inner temple. There is a strange music in the air. The ice breaks, crackles and sings, rhythmically composing a symphony of sound currents as a background to the mystical stillness that transports one to the misty dawn of this planet. I have felt as if I have stood at the edge of the world. This is where this earth ends or begins—it is the alpha and omega and feels like a gate into another dimension.

Returning from the polar cap, fantastic scenic wonders still await one. There is Magdalena Bay on Spitzbergen, one of the northernmost human habitations in the world. I have walked on the lovely beach there that is nestled at the foot of a narrow valley between awe-inspiring glaciers leading up into high mountains which tower over everything like watch guards patiently protecting this last piece of pure nature. I felt a little guilty invading this place along with some six hundred adventurous passengers. How did we dare to interfere with this untouched piece of land? But, just to step ashore in such majesty had the effect on many of feeling awe and wonder... at least for a few hours.

One of the park rangers who lived in a small hut by the water told us stories both happy and sad. Apparently, there is a strange woman living up here who has found inner peace in this incredible land. Alone in her silent bliss, she hunts for reindeer and salmon in order to survive. But, the ranger also told us about the two hunters who had pitched their tent in this valley. A hungry grizzly bear caught them preparing their breakfast in front of their tent. The huge animal grabbed one of the hunters, stood up on his hind feet and savagely ate the man before his companion's very eyes. After that story, most the passengers hastily returned to the safety of the ship!

For an entertainer on board one of these cruises, it is best to perform early in the voyage. The excitement of the extreme north with its eternal daylight causes a serious lack of sleep. Body clocks become transformed by the midnight sun and nobody goes to bed. Ships' bars are busy at three in the morning! As the ships enter into the second part of their voyage cruising in and out of the beautiful Norwegian fjords much further south, night returns. Passengers seek sleep, and enthusiasm for evening entertainment dwindles. I have sometimes played to an almost totally snoring audience. But, I don't mind. I often have encouraged them, telling them that it is my belief that if my music can relax the audience into sleep it is proving its healing sound! It helps, although I also ask them if they can manage to snore to the rhythm of the music (at least until I wake them up with an upbeat piccolo piece.)

Often when I am contracted on a North Cape cruise it includes a subsequent cruise through the Baltic Sea to St. Petersburg and back. The first time I went to Russia was with the Munich Bach Orchestra nearly thirty years ago. We played in Leningrad, which with the break up of communism in Russia has now reverted back to its original name of St. Petersburg. The tour also took the orchestra to Moscow.

The audiences in Russia were astounding. When the Munich Bach Orchestra played the *'B' Minor Mass* by J.S. Bach both in Moscow and in Leningrad, the Russian people would still be clapping in standing ovations for forty-five minutes after the performance. They gave us huge receptions with mountains of red caviar that always disappeared within twenty minutes as soon as the 140-member orchestra and choir had arrived!

The USSR was much more constrictive than modern-day Russia. As Westerners we weren't allowed to walk around or explore her cities, and I remember clearly that I got arrested because I walked around by myself in the harbor precincts of Leningrad. Now, however, a new cruise ship terminal has been built in this area and there are lots less restrictions, although not all the red tape has disappeared.

In the summer of 1995, I went into St. Petersburg alone. I shouldered a little backpack with one of my favorite stuffed animals, Dr. Crow, some papers, and some personal items, and set out for a day of adventure. I walked for miles. A highlight was my opportunity to visit the great museum of the Hermitage on my own. In the past I had only been able to visit what has to be one of the world's greatest treasure houses of fine art as well as the Winter Palace of the Russian Tsars, on a restricted "Intourist" tour. Such a visit can only scratch the surface of this unbelievable collection.

When I re-emerged hours later into the surrounding square, I noticed three or four horses tethered in the bright, clear sunlight. One stood out as being particularly beautiful with a white mane and tail. I don't speak Russian, but with universal sign language I asked, "Can I ride him?"

"Sure," came the motioned reply. The lady held up all her fingers to signify a price of ten rubles.

Gleefully, I climbed on and galloped around this historic square surrounded on three sides by some of St. Petersburg's most beautiful buildings and supporting in its midst Tsar Alexander I's free-standing monument commemorating the Russian defeat of Napoleon immortalized in Tschaikovsky's *1812 Overture*. Suddenly, a feeling I hadn't experienced in this lifetime flashed through me. Yet, it was such a familiar sensation. Something about the slanting sunlight, the air, and this location fused in my brain. A scatter shot of old images coursed through my mind's eye. As I rode, I drifted back into another time.

I glimpsed hordes of people standing in this very square. Their clothes were from another era. Horses and people were running toward the palace. Violent feelings hung on the air... a coup, perhaps during one of the revolutions. The vision or memory took my breath away. Slowly, I brought the ride to an end. As I dismounted, the experience faded. I leaned over the horse's neck and patted him.

Later, as I tried to analyze this I felt like I may have been a soldier on a horse in this frightening drama. I sensed it as a moment of great importance from my past—a haunting refrain in the melody that is I.

I was lost in time. The past-life glimpse shook my hold on every day matters. When I looked at my watch, I suddenly realized that my ship was leaving in an hour. I was still in the heart of the city far away from the port!

Panicking, I rooted through my backpack for the map given to me upon disembarkation. It gave the name of the port and directions back to the ship in Cyrillic. (They don't use an alphabet in Russia that we can read. It's like Japanese or Arabic. You have to know the exact spelling and lettering to ask for help.) This all-important piece of paper had vanished.

It was now clear to me that I was in trouble. Standing in the middle of this city lost in time, I began politely accosting people in English, German, French, Spanish, and even Portuguese. None of them could help me. I pulled out a picture postcard of the ship and pointed to it, but still there was no response.

Desperately, I started yelling to every passerby: "Do you know this ship?"

One older woman responded and motioned to me to follow her. My hopes were raised. After several streets she pointed proudly to a huge building: it was the Post Office! The woman thought I wanted to mail this card with the ship on it! My heart sank again. I could not communicate my need to return to the port. Now, I got really nervous. Sweat started to pour down my back. "If the ship leaves," I said to myself, "that's it. I will have to stay in Russia till I find another way out. It won't be easy to explain to the authorities how I got here. All my papers of identification along with my passport, are on the ship."

I sat down and took everything out of my backpack from gum wrappers to sunglasses, even the stuffed crow that is a favorite companion. "Where is the paper with the port name?" I asked Dr. Crow sadly. I started to cry as I squatted beside the messy pile of paperback books, music tapes, and wadded-up papers.

Unfortunately, Dr. Crow could offer no advice. "Try breathing, try chanting," I told myself, reminded of my feeling of despair in Rome when I was traveling with Kim. "Just breathe." Then, I started to softly hum "Hu," that ancient name for God, the chant that had helped me and uplifted me in the past. I relaxed a little and could breathe better. All of a sudden, I heard a voice: "What is that creature?" someone was saying in a strong Russian accent as they looked at Dr. Crow among my scattered possessions on the sidewalk. Before me stood a very handsome young man with kind eyes. "Can I help you?" he asked.

"Yes, indeed you can!" I shouted excitedly. "Thank God you speak English! I'm lost. I need to get back to the port. My ship is about to sail."

His dancing eyes returned to the stuffed crow. "How do you call it in English?" he asked.

Being more relaxed; I animated Dr., Crow. "I am a crow," I squawked, "I am really lost and need help."

The Russian gentleman smiled and immediately took a great interest in me since I had appealed to his sense of humor. In a matter of minutes, my new friend, Bogdan, had figured out where the ship was from my description. We jumped into a taxi, chattering all the way. Finally, we reached the ship about five minutes before they pulled up the gangway. Bogdan and I said "So long" at the terminal laughing and appreciating each other and our newly made friendship, which was ignited by a stuffed crow sitting on the sidewalk.

Anything can connect people—a smile, music, humor, a stuffed bear or even a crow can all act as a passkey to understanding and help. It works in all languages and all cultures. You do not really need many words to make someone laugh. Just be willing to laugh at yourself!

Standing at the railing, looking out over the water and seeing the beautiful city of the white nights disappear into a mirage on the horizon, I thanked that invisible energy which some call Spirit, others God or Divine Love, and which had guided me, through my toy companion Dr. Crow, to meet Bogdan. Since then, I have returned to St. Petersburg three times and each time I have managed to look up Bogdan. We celebrate our bond, which goes beyond all the differences in culture, language and background. I have also found the white horse waiting for me in the square. Perhaps his energy, too, was in that square when those angry crowds came by all those years ago! Soul's energies meet and awaken in each other. We are all of the same energy, and we can truly appreciate each other if we recognize this.

This experience was also a good reminder to me of the power of humor, and the need to relax and trust the flow of life. Whenever I do, things always turn out all right!

That night in the safe environment of my cabin, I thought back on an earlier visit to Leningrad. I'd accompanied Emanuil Sheynkman, the great balalaika player, to the city which had once been his home. Emanuil had emigrated with his family from the Soviet Union to the United States about ten years before. Having been one of the most famous and celebrated balalaikists in Russia for most of his life, he found himself in America in a totally different and musically challenging situation. He put it this way: "In Russia, all I had to worry about was my music; in America, I have to worry about business of music first." He had become a musical partner and dear friend of both Richard Patterson and myself. It was a particular thrill that we had managed to arrange a concert booking for the three of us on this ship's tour in the Baltic. After ten years in the States, Emanuil or Misha as we all called him was making his first return visit to his homeland and native city. Naturally, Misha wanted us to help him bring into Leningrad the countless gifts he had brought for all his friends. Along with some of the ship's musicians, we helped him lug these items through customs. There were blenders, assorted cosmetics, sneakers, coffee machines and even a trumpet for one of his musician friends. We all succeeded in passing through customs with this stuff, even the trumpet made it. Misha, knowing the Russian system well, had written up a fake dedication certificate purportedly from an American professor, which stated that this was a very special gift for the Russian musician. It worked. The power of the written word impressed the customs officer. Then, we all accompanied Misha to Pushkin Plaza where his many friends stood waiting. It was a very moving scene: everybody embraced with Russian bear hugs, tears in their eyes. We also cried. They were tears of joy.

I left Emanuil to his friends and started walking back to the ship with a big smile on my face. Along the way, I met a young couple who spoke English. We got along famously enjoying a long conversation as they fell into step to walk me back to the port area. Before we parted I asked them: "Is there anything you would like from the ship?"

"Yes, there is one great convenience item you could provide," the young Russian woman suggested. "Disposable diapers for our baby! It would make it so much easier to travel in the car," they enthused. "We could visit department stores, and have more freedom with our baby!"

I told them to wait for me on the dock as I ran aboard to find the Chief Purser. He helped me to locate a large package of hundreds of disposable diapers that was in the ship's hospital. I offered to pay for them, but the Doctor and the Purser insisted that I took them as a free gift to my Russian friends. To be truthful, there was not much need for this commodity on board the ship and the Doctor was glad to be rid of at least part of this package that was taking up valuable locker space.

Excitedly, I grabbed a few dozen and disembarked to go through customs with my large parcel. This time, they stopped me. Even though I had passed before with many items, they wanted to know what was in this particular package. After close inspection, they still couldn't understand what I was carrying. I explained the merits of disposable diapers as carefully as I could in broken English.

Finally, some understanding dawned. With a look of pity, the customs agents let me pass. They thought I had a medical problem— that I couldn't go anywhere without tons of these disposable diapers! I started laughing myself silly as I explained their impression to the young couple waiting for me beyond the restricted area.

"Didn't you say you just brought all kinds of things through customs for Emanuil's friends?" they asked.

"Yes," I confirmed, still laughing, "and they never stopped me. Rather grimly, they just waved me through. Isn't it funny? This time they gave me lots more compassion and they actually smiled." We all laughed together.

The couple was in ecstasy. Now, they could tote their baby to all kinds of new places in comfort. Suddenly, in the midst of our laughter, I felt that same chill I had experienced galloping around the square. I thought I knew these people from a past life. They were so hauntingly familiar. Maybe travel can be an expression of divine guidance. You have the opportunity to connect with so many souls that may have touched you in the past that without travel you might never meet. Maybe the disposable diapers were an opportunity to return a favor from long, long ago.

My thoughts drifted to all my friends in Russia, those that I had met and those that I feel I still may meet. I have this strange affinity with Russia. I thought of the white horse that I have now ridden several times around the Hermitage. He probably went home that night and said to the other horses at his stable: "Guess what? I had that woman on my back again today—the one who was here two years ago! The one whom I remember from the days of the revolution when I was a handsome black stallion." It's a wonderful feeling to be reminded that life is much larger than we can fathom. Spirit moves in so many mysterious ways. I feel very much part of a larger picture, secure in my feeling that I have lived here before and grateful for the transforming encounters that I have experienced in this most beautiful place, Peter the Great's window on the world and Russia's city of white nights.

I returned from the Baltic on a transatlantic crossing via Iceland thus completing my tour through the Nordic countries. As we approached this incredible land of rugged mountains, volcanoes and thermal springs, we passed one of the planet's most recent miracles, Surtsey Island. Just over twenty years ago, Surtsey rose from the sea as a volcanic cone spewing lava and fire. Today, it is a green island of grasses and simple wild flowers and a home to thousands of birds. Many of the ship's passengers came out on deck to see this wonder of contemporary geological creation.

As the ship approached Reykjavik, Iceland's capital, we could see the long sweep of mountains on a narrow peninsula jutting out into the sea that form Reykjavik Bay. They culminate in Iceland's equivalent of Mount Fuji—an incredible perfectly formed cone its upper reaches covered in pristine white snow.

This was my first visit to Iceland and the island fascinated me. I had always longed to see the land that bred the horses of my childhood. It was from here that Svadi's ancestors had come. Icelandic horses have five gaits instead of three. They have this special gait which is smooth for traveling long distances called "Toelt." Naturally, I wanted to ride Icelandic horses while I was there. I found a riding stable and arranged to rent five horses for the day, as three of the dancers from the Production Group on board along with the wonderful harpist Andrea Stern wanted to accompany me. Even though it was late summer, it was very cold because of a biting wind. We rode out looking like firemen in rubber jackets and helmets that we had borrowed from the ship.

There are few trees in Iceland, but there are wide grass valleys crisscrosssed with little ravines between the ridges of mountain ranges. In such a valley, not far from Reykjavik, we saw the sight of the first parliament in the world. Then, leaving history behind, we headed out into the wild beauty beyond. We rode for almost four hours and I started to worry a bit about the dancers and the harpist as none of them had ever ridden before. But, the beauty of the land was overcoming any worry over sore bottoms or knees!

Despite the Icelandic gait of our magnificent horses, however, we all had stiff muscles on returning to the ship. It had been a great adventure, very cold, somewhat uncomfortable, but exciting.

Unfortunately for the dancers, they had to perform a show opener that night. They were barely able to walk out on stage during the blackout; however, as it goes in their profession, once the lights were on them and the band struck up, their adrenaline took over. Only I was aware of their predicament, but when I went backstage after their performance, my three riding companions had collapsed in agony. Fortunately, I was able to rest, but not before seeing us sail out of the harbor leaving behind one of our planet's most beautiful and mysterious islands.

I spent much of the remaining passage to New York just staring at the ocean. It is good for the soul, I believe, to just take some time off, breathe unpolluted air and contemplate on the beauty of our world, as we all had when we started this voyage sailing up into the polar cap north of Norway. The sound of silence had been all around. As I gazed at the ocean, I sensed that same interconnectedness in this vast space. We were close to the spot where the *Titanic* sank in April of 1912. I couldn't help but reflect on the most recent and extraordinary award-winning film about this event. Despite all the horrors of that fateful April night, James Cameron somehow managed to capture the beauty, too, not only in the romantic love story of Rose and Jack, but in the fleeting moments that revealed the majesty of the heavens above the dark sea from which millions of crystal clear stars twinkled, or that moment of pink dawn when the rescue ship *Carpathia* arrived and the majesty of the very ice that had destroyed the *Titanic* reflected the dawn's light in a thousand prisms.

In my show on this section of the Trans-Atlantic crossing, I played my composition *Love Song for the Water Planet*. When we reached Bar Harbor, Maine, en route to New York, I took a walk up the main street of this quaint town. I noticed a harp store... rather unusual, so I ducked in to look at some of their Celtic and Irish harps. Like many such stores, they sold some nature CD's and a number of specialist artists' recordings on instruments such as flute and harp. While I was looking through these CD's, a woman whom I had never seen before, came to the shop's counter. "Do you have a recording called *Love Song to a Planet*?" she asked.

"Who recorded it?" the summer student managing the till replied.

"It was recorded by the Celtic harpist Kim Robertson," the woman answered. "The flutist was Bettine Clemen."

The student looked up some papers. "We should have it over there," she said pointing at the rack where I was.

There was my recording *Love Song to a Planet* right before my eyes. I picked a copy up and handed it to the lady with a smile. The woman thanked me and turned the CD over to look at the back cover. She saw my photograph and looked up. She recognized me. "Isn't this you?" she asked with surprise. "You must be Bettine Clemen."

"I am," I replied. "Let me sign this for you."

This simple exchange gave me the necessary confirmation that my music and my work were indeed helping and touching others. I was assured that I am able to bring the mysterious majesty of our planet, such as I had recently witnessed in Norway and Iceland, and over the years in countless other places around the world including those rain forests of Brazil, to many people who do not have the travel opportunities that have come my way. This caused me great joy.

# Chapter Thirteen

# Travels to Africa and India

In recent years weather patterns seem to have become more severe. Some see this as a signal of earth changes; others quietly blame all on 'El Nino.' Often these weather patterns cause problems for professional travelers like me. We become stranded for days in airports—sleeping on floors, losing our luggage, complaining and moaning. Schools are closed much to the delight of children. Businesses and banks sometimes close, and often, severe weather causes the temporary shutdown of some government-provided services.

If these are times of change, and many think so as we approach the Millennium, these are also times of great opportunities for quantum leaps in consciousness. Any crisis can be an opportunity for growth as we help others in our common plight. During one of these severe weather patterns I started a concert tour around the world via six different cruise liners and several connecting flights.

Leaving the winter snows in Minnesota, I arrived in the warm sunshine of the Caribbean to sail on board the *Vistafjord*. But, on Antigua and Montserrat I saw the scars of recent hurricanes. What was once the image of paradise for tourists all over the world had been transformed into a disaster area. Houses were ripped apart and blown away, shopping centers flattened, trees and bushes uprooted. Many people and pets were homeless. Nevertheless, nature had come back in its powerful way with remarkable speed, and the regenerating grass and seedlings looked even greener than before.

Montserrat was a beautiful lush green island, which had been in the news much of the previous year. The island's volcano had become active again, with sulfurous smoke and gasses spewing out of its crater. The locals told me that they were evacuated three times, once in September to the island of Antigua, where they were then hit by a hurricane. But, most of them had insisted on coming back to their homes and rebuilding all over again.

A few days later, I arrived in Dakar, Africa, thousands of miles from the Caribbean yet in another kind of turmoil. But, this is normal for the area. It has always been that way. It was from here that slaves were shipped to the Americas having been sold by their tribal chiefs for a pittance. A visit to Goree Island is a swift reminder of man's inhumanity to man. There is an interesting West African mesh of Arab and African, French colonial and tribal in the total chaos of Dakar's streets. People yell and scream and there are unbelievable smells, but there are also beautiful and intense colors and graceful, tall, dark people.

I was traveling with my husband Peter, and a male classical guitarist, George Sakellariou. Our adventure started near the end of our short visit to Dakar with a taxi ride from our hotel to the ship on which we were to sail. Between us we had six heavy suitcases.

Two taxi drivers in long flowing caftans arrived to pick us up. One screamed with bombastic authority, "The woman comes with me, and the two men go with the other cab!"

I took one look at him, 'No way Jose!' I thought before jumping into the other cab with my husband. Who knows where I would have ended up? White slavery is not outside the realm of possibility. A scene came into my mind from my last tour to Tangiers, Morocco.

As three female musician friends and I were walking through the narrow, dark and smelly streets of the old bazaar area in Tangiers, a voice yelled out at us. Turning, I saw a man pointing at me. He seriously announced to his friend: "That blond woman we can sell for ten thousand camels!"

I started walking much faster, even though the truth be known I felt somewhat flattered. I was sure nobody had ever offered that much for me! But, I did not intend to spend the rest of my life in a harem in Morocco. Peter had told me about a secretary of his who had once been abducted in Morocco. It does happen!

This scene outside our hotel in Dakar seemed to show all the hallmarks of abduction danger. The cab driver muttered obscenities because I had not followed his instructions and there followed loud yelling and screaming over money. Eventually the cab started toward the harbor. Three times the driver brought us to a halt. Finally, venting his anger, he stopped in the middle of a totally chaotic street and emphatically unloaded all our baggage. He wanted still more money. Peter refused to negotiate with him and started to put our bags back into the car. There was further abuse and spitting before the driver continued on his way eventually bringing us to our destination. Boy! Did that ship look good!

About ten young boys then grabbed at our luggage and I had to yell at them long and hard not to grab my flutes. It was with great relief that we finally climbed the gangway to enter the cool air-conditioning of the *Sagafjord*, the ship that would be our home for the next leg of our journey to South Africa.

Our next port of call was Walvis Bay in Namibia which was very much developed by South Africans, and for a small port town on the fringe of Africa's second largest desert has a surprising ring of prosperity. It is easy from Walvis Bay to drive into the desert for a day. Most people don't get beyond the initial sand dunes along the coast, which are impressive, but to drive on into the desert heart is a different kind of experience. Here again can be heard the sound of silence. I don't think that the sound current that connects us with the planet has ever rung as strongly in my ears as in the stillness of Namibia. The silence was deafening, an extraordinary illusion but a great lesson. Open your ears in such silence, for there is nothing in Namibia to disturb the total peace, and the music of the universe plays for you... the music of our divine awareness. It is as if you are hearing the very atoms that form the Universe and unite us all in a common bond of matter and divinity. My ears rang for days from that experience.

Likewise, in the game parks of Kenya one can sense the "big country" where the land meets the sky in an extraordinary union that is divine. Perhaps, outside Africa, this same experience can best be sensed in the outback of Australia's red center and it is not surprising that mankind's oldest civilization, the aborigines, once had such a strong understanding of the bonding between all life forms and the land. Where you can hear the mysterious sound current of divine connection it becomes easy to understand this philosophy of interconnection.

The bustling Kenyan port of Mombassa lies almost right across the continent from the West African ports between Dakar and Walvis Bay. There is both a heavy Arab and Indian influence in this one time bastion of Portuguese and British colonial Africa. This is the port of entry for visiting those fabled game parks—Tsarvo and Masai Mara being the most accessible. A world of wild nature, threatened by the upset ecology of Africa created by false, man-made nations and past colonial policies of commercial greed, awaits the traveler. There are still lions, cheetahs, zebra, eland, elephants and giraffes to see. The vast skies and massive landscape still beckons. But, one has to wonder for how much longer. Africa is in turmoil.

Many Indian families travel on board ships that make annual crossings between India and East Africa. It is a short and colorful period when these passengers board in Bombay (Mumbai) or Madras (Chennai.) As this is a relatively short segment of any World Cruise they are generally considered by full world cruise passengers to be 'ferry boat' clientele, but they certainly leave their mark. These ships become ablaze with color as the Indian ladies grace the public rooms with their magnificent saris and punjabis.

In Mombassa I was staying with Peter at the *White Sands Resort* after the *QE2* had made such a crossing from Bombay to Mombassa. Many of the Indian passengers who had boarded in Bombay were also staying at the *White Sands Resort*. As we sat at sunset time watching dusk descend on the warm Indian Ocean, we observed one of these Indian families. Ravi had traveled on the *QE2* with his wife and two daughters. His daughters were full of life force with mischievous sparkling eyes. They had just dismounted from a sunset camel ride along the beach. Peter was fascinated, as he witnessed one of the camels at rest stretch out its long neck and place its head upon the sand. In Peter's novel *Legacy of a Star*, there is an important scene whereby a camel rests its head on the desert sands to be stung by a scorpion. This action starts a chain of reactions of importance in the story, but Peter had never seen a camel put its head down on the sand. He considered it a possibility that camels are like African giraffes that never put their heads down to rest. He researched this matter with a library in Chicago and when they sent him twenty pages on the sleeping habits of camels he learned to his delight that although it is not commonplace for a camel to lower its head onto the ground, there are times when they do so. Thus, the scene stayed in *Legacy of a Star*, but this confirmation of the reality on the beach in Mombassa greatly relieved his mind.

Ravi and his family took us to a restaurant in the hotel, which had been taken over by all the Indian passengers from the *QE2*. They were dressed in their finest seated out on this open verandah and celebrating a birthday. They welcomed us so much into their presence treating us as guests of honor. We had the most wonderful evening and our friendship with Ravi and his family grew deeper.

The following year we visited Ravi in Bombay. He would do anything for us. He even said he would make arrangements for us to travel to Nepal or Ladakh, which we had discussed as a personal desire. We were entertained royally at his house where I played a concert for his friends. Ravi also played the flute, but Ravi was a sort of Indian Renaissance man. He admitted he needed to work on his flute playing, but he introduced me to some of the haunting beauty of Indian music.

Ravi was a rich man; he had inherited great wealth from his father, a very successful businessman in Bombay. He had a personal fleet of eight cars and owned no less than ten houses and at each maintained a retinue of servants. Peter and I went with him to one of his homes across the murky waters of Bombay harbor along the mainland coast. This was a private rural area where several wealthy Indians had hideaway homes. Ravi's ranch home was surrounded by perfumed gardens, even if like most places in India, it was somewhat chaotic. There was a huge swimming pool in which we swam before sitting with Ravi discussing ancient Indian philosophy. We sat on wicker chairs that were carried out by the servants as in those old photographs of the days of the British Raj.

The servants were always close by. Ravi would clap his hands. "Patma!" he would shout. "Bring Bettine some more tea. Bring Peter more juice," or "Ramu," who was his chauffeur bearer, "Bring Bettine to the stables." And so it would go on all day. There was always a servant within earshot standing on duty in the shade of a tree. It was something to which Peter and I were not used and it took us some time to realize that even the milk for the cereal had to be poured by either Patma or one of the other six or seven house servants.

The next morning we arose at sunrise to visit Ravi's neighbor, an equally wealthy Indian gentleman who loved horses. Soon, we were riding thoroughbreds on the beach feeling the freedom of peace and contentment.

Because Ravi expounded philosophy, we called him Swami Ravi. Actually, Ravi was no Guru—He was a seeker. He was in his quiet way wrestling with himself to solve the riddle of life. Two days later, after Peter had left me to sail from Bombay on the *QE2*, Ravi took me up to Poona where we visited the ashram founded by Osho also known as Bhagwan Rajneesh, who had been one of the most controversial teachers during his earth stay. I am not an Osho follower even though I have read several of his thought provoking books, but it was a wonderful experience for me as I sensed the interconnectedness of all those who had gathered here from many nations of the world. One does not need a Guru and I do not believe that this particular ashram was intended to be a rigid spiritual experience. They had established a "Multiversity" instead of a "University" where one could explore and study a multitude of approaches, such as Zen Buddhism, Yoga, Christian mysticism, past life regression, meditation, Tai Chi, martial arts, breathing and many more. The joy of Osho's teaching was its universal appeal encouraging us to seek and become our own masters.

As I reflected on my wonderful experiences in Poona and Bombay, and the great generosity and love that I felt from Ravi and his family, I could not help but recall the negative comments of some passengers about their fellow Indian guests. In truth, Ravi and his family could probably have bought out most of the rich Westerners traveling on board, but although their lives were in an Indian India that aped the social structures of the once British Raj, Ravi and his family were not materially minded. Despite their many servants, dust lay thick on their furniture. It was not their wealth that made them Maharajahs, but their inner shining light.

# Chapter Fourteen

# Pacific Kava

During the past five or six years, I have traveled consistently through the winter months on various ships circumnavigating the globe. In the profession we call this "ship jumping." My agent makes the bookings and the shipping lines work out with him how to fly me around the world from one ship to another in the most economical way. Winter world cruises are a little different from the summer voyages in the Mediterranean and northern Europe and very different from Caribbean cruises and the now very commercial Alaska trade. Richard and I used to play Classical concerts on Alaska cruises in the 1980's when this magnificent terrain really was still America's last frontier, and I'm glad that I had the experience back then. The beauty of that waterway from Ketchichan to Russian Sitka was the inspiration for some of our best music together including Richard's very special composition *Inside Passage*. But, these days some thirty ships ply Alaska's inside passage during the summer months and places like Juneau and Skagway have developed with the same honky-tonk rapidity as they did in the original days of the Alaskan Gold Rush. I now prefer to concentrate my cruising concerts on the winter months and to work primarily on festivals and events on land during the summer.

World cruises usually sail from East to West to make the time changes easier on the passengers. Leaving from the United States, therefore, it is the vast Pacific Ocean that gives one the first real taste of the coming adventure. Ports are less frequent, scattered between long lazy days on the world's largest ocean. One can easily understand why we call our planet "The Water Planet." I know from first-hand experience that seventy percent of this planet is covered by water... water... nothing but water and the huge sky above it. This undisturbed horizon is the cause for those legendary Pacific sunsets and that eternal quest for the moment of the 'green' flash—a scientific phenomenon that shows the greens from the disappearing spectrum of the sun's rays as it sets beyond the visual limits of the ocean. The vast vistas of ocean are what I enjoy most on these world cruises. As experienced returning from Europe on the North Atlantic, they are very soothing for the soul. I always come away with fresh spiritual insights. When one looks out from the railing of these large ships carrying seven hundred to twelve hundred passengers, our moving body appears quite small and insignificant compared to the vastness of the great Pacific Ocean. Among my greatest experiences on these Pacific meanderings has been to stand at the foremost point of the bow, just like Jack and Rose in the film *Titanic*, and feel the wind on my face as I fly into the sunset. This experience is not usually available to passengers, but as an entertainer I travel as a crewmember. The foredeck is one of those areas of a ship that is most often off limits to passengers, but used as a promenade and recreation area by crewmembers. I can genuinely testify to the incredible sensation of flying from the bow railing, but I have to admit that there is a big difference to experiencing this in the balmy warmth of the Pacific rather than what must have been perishing cold April conditions on the North Atlantic for James Cameron's fictitious hero and heroine.

Usually on these tours my schedule is fairly light. As a featured performer, I will probably play a total of three, fifty-minute shows over a ten day period. There will be plenty of time between rehearsals and daily practice to breathe in the pure, invigorating sea air, and to simply be in this wondrous water world.

Each day, I meet at least one interesting person. It could be a fellow lecturer or entertainer, a passenger who strikes up a conversation, or one of the on-board clergy members. On a world cruise most ships carry a Roman Catholic priest, a Protestant clergyman, and a rabbi. Often they get together for Inter-denominational and Inter-Faith worship. I have had many wonderful encounters with these representatives of various religions. At sea there seems to be a great kinship between all spiritually minded people. They tend to group together to share what they hold in common, instead of concentrating on mundane differences. At the same time, there seems to be a greater appreciation for all differences, whether they are in color, race or religion. The crewmembers of the *QE2* for instance come from thirty-six different nations and they have to find a way to all get along. They are literally all in the same boat—a microcosm of the world or a mini-version of the United Nations!

On a recent voyage, I met a Roman Catholic priest named Father Michael. He was filled with so much joy and bubbling energy and uplifted everybody with his mere presence. My Celtic harpist friend Kim and I spent most of our time with Father Michael. We ate together and laughed a lot. He asked us to play some solos for his daily Mass. It didn't matter that we were not Catholic... not even practicing Christians! We enjoyed each other as divine sparks of God, or soul.

I will never forget the day before we were due to leave that particular cruise. Father Michael came to our room, which was more like a suite. This was a very luxurious ship and every entertainer got a huge double-cabin with a picture window and among other things, a totally stocked bar.

Father Michael went straight to our refrigerator and asked; "Now you girls, do you still have all that booze they gave you with the room?"

Puzzled, Kim and I replied in unison, "Yes." We shrugged our shoulders at each other as he looked in the refrigerator. Was this some kind of religious test of purity? Neither of us drank!

"Well, you see," Father Michael explained looking back at us with a face that would have been well at home in an Irish bar, "I want to give all those bottles to the poor people at our next port of call!"

The priest left with as many bottles as his arms could carry. Halfway down the aisle of the corridor, he turned around and winked at us. "Boy, I sure hope I don't run into the Rabbi carrying all this!"

On a Tahiti bound cruise out of Honolulu on board the *Vistafjord* I was also lucky to be given a premier cabin. I had my own piece of sky and sea, in the form of a private balcony—a rare occurrence.

After I had performed my first show, I was walking around the deck to unwind before retiring for the night. A terrific thumping noise startled me. Something, or someone, had crashed into the wall over my head. I turned to see a huge bird falling backward onto the deck. It must have flown into a window.

The bird and I both trembled as I approached. His large, curved beak could easily snap a finger or two. His feathers were jet-black and he was bigger than the largest raven and had webbed, sea-going feet. He looked too strong to tackle alone.

Stumbling in my long sequined gown and heels, I ran back into the ballroom for help. When I emerged with two Filipino stewards in tow, the bird was floundering about in the bottom of the empty swimming pool. The night cleaning crew had just drained it. The stewards chased my bird around the pool for a bit with no success. Finally, I threw off my heels and climbed down the steep ladder myself. Fortunately, most the passengers were in bed thus missing this circus.

It was difficult to get anywhere near the shaking bird. I tried singing and chanting softly to calm us both. 'Fill yourself with unconditional love,' I thought to myself. 'Let a melody flow forth.' Slowly the bird stopped flapping and closed its eyes. One of the stewards threw me a towel and I wrapped him up, getting a wicked bite or two in the process—but, now what?

One of my colleagues, a cellist, came outside to see what all the commotion was about. After laughing good and hard, she told me: "You've bagged a frigate bird. Put him in my bathtub for the night."

I reminded her that this would not be a popular arrangement with the ship's authorities. I remembered what trouble my imaginary thirty birds from *Love Song to a Planet* had caused. Only the magician had permission to bring birds aboard ship, and that was after months of special paper work, quarantines, and permission from all the ports of call, but we took the bird to her cabin in any case.

In the morning, the cellist and I decided to move the stowaway to my balcony for fresh air. I let my kindly stewardess in on the secret, but asked her to keep quiet about it. Later, my friend and I fed the stowaway bird fresh shrimp and sushi from the five-star midnight buffet. This became one pampered bird! The waiters gave me strange looks as I sneaked outside with a loaded plate each night.

Unfortunately, the bird didn't eat much—he trembled non-stop at his strange circumstances and usually took only a little water. One leg and wing seemed to droop as if injured. At times I played Tibetan flute to calm him.

Finally, the ship arrived at Aitutaki, in French Polynesia. We decided to take the bird ashore.

I felt it best to take him in a cardboard box. He seemed stronger, but still very shy. With some struggle and a few pecks, we managed to stuff him inside. Naturally, I was elected to nonchalantly carry this huge container to the tender boat that ferries passengers ashore. I gingerly took my place in the boat, hoping no one would ask about the box. Unfortunately, two officials from the island planted themselves in front of me in the boat. "What is in that box?" they demanded.

I turned all kinds of shades of red. "A bird," I blurted out. Talking fast, I explained as best I could the story of how I had taken care of the bird.

"No way," they each said firmly. "It's not allowed. The bird might bring disease to this island."

"How can it, when it's from your ocean!" I protested.

"What kind of bird is it?" one asked curiously.

"Never mind," his colleague reminded him. "It's not allowed."

"Do you want to see?" I replied beguilingly, "It wants to come out anyway."

One of the officials foolishly stuck his hand in the box, only to get pecked at rather badly. This made him angry. "You must stay in the tender boat and return to the ship with the bird," he pronounced. "You can't land here with that bird."

Obediently, but sadly, I returned to the ship on the same tender after the passengers had landed on Aitutaki. As we approached the *Vistafjord* I was smarting tears not knowing what I would do with the bird. The Hotel Manager, who was sitting not far from me in the open stern area of the small boat, noticed my sadness and came over to sit beside me. I admit that this act of kindness actually made me a little nervous as I knew I was not supposed to have a bird in my cabin on board added to which the Hotel Manager might have heard something about my bird from the immigration and customs officers who had just got off the tender as he had got on. The Hotel Manager runs the daily affairs of the ship as one of the four-stripe officers under the Captain. He could easily decide to bump me to a lesser cabin without my balcony and never invite me to play again. But, the Austrian-born Hotel Manager, Englebert Lainer, had always been very friendly toward me having been brought up near the Lake Chiemsee area of my childhood. I gathered up all my courage.

"Englebert, there's a bird in this box," I told him in German. "They won't let me take him over to the island. I don't know what to do."

The man smiled incredulously. "What? How? Never mind... I don't want to know. But, why take him to the island? He's a bird—why don't you just set him free?" he chuckled. But, he saw that I was crying and was moved by my compassion for the bird. I told him my story. "Let me help you," he said. "Let's see if the bird can fly."

I agreed and we stood up looking out over the stern back toward the island and opened the box.

The minute the lid lifted, my black friend shot away and flew non-stop for six or seven minutes before disappearing from view. Englebert and I were both filled with the inexplicable joy of the bird's freedom. Englebert turned to me with tears in his own eyes—a very unusual occurrence for this strong officer of the sea.

"That bird meant a lot to you, didn't it?" he said. We were both touched and amused to see this frigate bird fly straight toward the very island to which the French Polynesian officials had said I couldn't take it.

That night, my fellow musicians, and even the room stewardess inquired after the bird and rejoiced with me in its freedom. Of course, I wasn't quite as joyful when I had to scrub the balcony free of the many memorabilia he had left—it was hard work. But, as I scrubbed I suddenly had a funny image of this bird returning to his family. "Where have you been?" they might ask him. "I took a cruise," he might well have replied. "Oh, you wouldn't believe it. I sailed on a five-star ship. They fed me seven-course meals and serenaded me with Tibetan-flute concerts. I can recommend it very highly."

I hoped, however, that the bird had opened its heart to our love. I know that those of us who had taken care of him felt that he had opened our hearts.

Pago Pago, pronounced Pango Pango, is beyond Tahiti and a last American outpost on a conventional voyage across the Pacific. Beyond, are the islands of Tonga and Fiji and the greater islands of New Zealand and continental Australia. Pago Pago is just about in the middle of the Pacific Ocean. Popular anthropological theory suggests that it was here from these Samoan islands that the great canoes of the Polynesian peoples moved out northeast and southwest to bring Polynesian culture to Hawaii and New Zealand. But, how did the Polynesians get to Samoa in the middle of the Pacific ocean in the first place? Possibly they came from South America as Thor Hyderdhal tried to prove with his building of the balsa wood raft *Kontiki*, but it is equally as likely that they journeyed from South East Asia over millennia. It is one of those fascinating mysteries, insights on which are given to cruise passengers by enlightened lecturers that accompany world cruise ships.

American Samoa is usually hot... very hot. I recall it having been one hundred degrees on one of my visits as I used this American outpost to make some final calls to my home in Minneapolis, Minnesota. That same day it was minus forty degrees up there! I offered to send them at least fifty degrees of Pago Pago's sweltering heat! That would have brought Minneapolis to just a little above freezing and eased some of the winter pain!

A short visit in a drugstore on my way back to the ship presented me with an interesting insight into some young Samoans' goals. I met several teens in the store as Peter and I picked up supplies of sunblock and some aspirins. When we mentioned the beauty and peace of the islands, they demurred, "All we want to do is leave here and live in the big cities in America!" The age-old story of the grass being greener on the other side is alive everywhere. I was reminded that paradise is truly an inner state rather than an outer condition.

On this occasion traveling with us on board the *Royal Viking Sun* to Fiji where he has a wonderful ecological resort, was our friend Jean-Michel Cousteau. He was on board as one of those enlightened guest speakers. His presentations are always filled with much knowledge and a great sincerity and dedication to the preservation of the planet for future generations. "What kind of a world are we leaving behind us?" is an urgent question that he always asks his audiences to consider.

In his final talk of the cruise, Jean-Michel described an event in Arizona, where he had the opportunity to talk to 11,000 young people between 10 and 16 years old.

"It was really scary at first," he admitted in his wonderful French accent. "I thought I would faint right there surrounded by thousands of kids in this huge basketball arena. But, then it all seemed to come together when I tried to make a pact with them. I asked them to sit down at least once a week for a real family dinner—one without the TV blaring out, so that they really could talk to their families... discuss their concerns about their personal lives, and about their environment; stay in touch with those who love them, just as we must stay in touch with Mother Earth. Then, in response, they suggested that we have a huge hug for the earth... 11,000 kids hugging. I have never experienced anything like it. If we can reach these young people and awaken in them an awareness about the preciousness of life on this planet, we will have better future leaders to take care of our world."

We landed at Savusavu in Fiji and visited the Jean-Michel Cousteau Fiji Island Resort shortly after it had opened. We were invited to spend the whole day in this unspoiled environment. It was very peaceful to walk along the virgin coastline. All one could hear was the sound of the wind in the palm trees and the music of the ocean.

At the resort, the traditional Fijian Kava ceremony took place. Kava is made from the root of a pepper plant that is pounded and then mixed with water. The men often sit around a big Kava bowl for many hours. A smaller bowl is also filled and passed to everyone in the circle. Once offered this, you must empty it in one gulp.

On this occasion, the chief of the village on whose lands the resort is situated spent all day at the Kava bowl.

What effect does the Kava have? Well, I was to find out! After a wonderful Fijian dinner followed by a spectacular spear dance, Jean-Michel asked me to play a few pieces. I decided to play the piece that I had dedicated to Jean-Michel and his work, *Love Song for the Water Planet*. Normally, the flute is accompanied not only by harp, but also by recorded birds from the Amazon rain forest. On this occasion, however, some of the local birds in the trees of the resort, responded to my flute and joined in. It was a magical moment.

As soon as the last note faded, the heavens opened. We experienced the most intense thunderstorm I have ever seen. It started to pour rain and the lightning and thunder that followed was like a vehement outburst of the energies of the skies. But, with great reverence, despite all that was going on around us, the Kava bowl was moved under a thatched roof and the ceremony continued.

I was invited to join the circle. I accepted it as an honor and when the small bowl was offered to me, I drank the muddy-looking stuff just as they had... in one gulp! It wasn't that bad, just a bit bitter. And of course, I had to put any thoughts of unhygienic germs totally out of my mind!

The Fijians were genuine and sincere in their offerings of friendship. I felt deeply moved as we sat and clapped our hands after each draught of the liquid 'mud.' All of us had wonderful smiles. We started to sing as the Kava bowl was offered again and again.

Then, after the exchange of some small gifts, the last boat came to take us back to our ship. It was magical to walk through the rain to the pier. The ship's tender brought us home to our floating hotel amid roaring peals of thunder. The Kava began to have a startling effect. I felt strange, but went to bed and hoped for the best. My dreams were really vivid and bizarre. When I awoke the following day, I felt very mellow. The only side effect seemed to be that my lips were numb.

This is not ideal for a flutist! Thank God the numbness disappeared just an hour before my evening show! I couldn't help thinking that maybe Father Michael would have enjoyed the Kava!

# Chapter Fifteen

# *Down Under*

Crossing the Pacific on board the *Royal Viking Sun* bound for Australia one winter, I shared a table in the ship's restaurant with a famous actor, singer, and composer from the good old days of "Hollywood." He was accompanying a ten-member "Broadway" cast to put on a show. One morning, between fruit, eggs, cereal and some of his awful-smelling cigarillos, he started to talk about his life and childhood.

"My parents both died rather suddenly," he explained. "First my mother was killed by a tractor and then my father died of illness very soon after," he reflected sadly. "But, when I was sitting at my father's deathbed, he suddenly pointed to the ceiling and whispered to me: 'Look at that light!' When I looked up, I saw it, too... a bright, white, pulsating light. Then, my father called out my mother's name: 'Help me across, my love, help me across!' he pleaded. This celebrity actor then paused for a moment looking straight at me, and smiled. "My father took his last breath with the most peaceful and serene expression I ever saw in him," he explained. "Since then, I know death is not to be feared!"

Here I was sitting with a "Hollywood" veteran who had seen the best times of film producing and had himself made many films with stars like Marilyn Monroe; he had lived for years in what to many people is seen as an artificial world best expressed on the front pages of the *National Enquirer*. But now, for the remaining years of his life he had left "Hollywood" to work with children and share his memories in a positive way.

He recited for me the lyrics to one of Peter Walker's songs, which I had enjoyed so much in his show and which expresses in a very direct and simple way a profound truth about life. It's called, "You Gotta Put Something in to Get Something Out."

> You put a seed in the ground and it grows,
> You put a breath in the wind and it blows!
> You put some ice in the rain and it snows,
> You gotta put something in to get something out!
> You put a star in the sky and it blinks,
> You put a thought in your brain and it thinks!
> You put your eye on a girl and it winks,
> You gotta put something in to get something out!
> You can take and take and take,
> But yet until you learn to give, you'll never get.
> You put some milk in a churn and it creams,
> You put a shine on the brass and it gleams,
> You put your head in a cloud and it dreams,
> You gotta put something in to get something out!

My friend may be unabashedly "Hollywood," but he also knows a few of the best secrets of life.

After a few more wondrous days in "Water World," we landed in Townsville, Australia, not so very far from the area along the Queensland coast where Captain Cook made a forced landing when his bark *Endeavour* was wrecked on the Great Barrier Reef. Here, I said farewell to my actor friend. After a brief land tour in Brisbane and a four-day break with my husband at Bedarra Island on the Barrier Reef, I would fly to Melbourne with Peter and sail to Bali on board the venerable old *Rotterdam*, now taken out of Holland-America service.

It was cooking-hot in Queensland, and we eagerly awaited an arranged visit to the rain forest, if nothing else but to experience the shade of the trees. The small bus taking us there climbed for two hours into the mountains before we finally got out to walk. What a delight! The temperature had dropped about fifteen degrees! As we set off down a trail, the exhilarating smells and sounds of the jungle engulfed and enthralled us.

Our guide explained the danger of getting lost in this vast rain forest. "Several people disappeared last year and were never found again," he informed us in his candid Aussie accent. "So please do not leave the path. As soon as you do, everything starts to look the same and in a small area you could be lost for days! Also, you might run into the Emu. If he thinks you are in his territory, he might rip your front open and then leave your corpse to rot! They don't attack for food, just territorial control."

After such insights, everyone indeed stayed on the path! The symphony of the bird sounds and the musky smells totally rejuvenated my body, mind, and spirit. I felt so grateful to all the living beings in this magical natural world! Mankind has intruded and mistreated our planet, yet it continues to give out its splendor—at least here in Australia, where the Queensland rain forests are now protected and have been re-seeded and replanted after earlier brutal rape by timber-hungry humans.

After this I spent those four days with Peter on one of the Great Barrier Reef Island resorts. It was a wonderful experience, being one of the more remote and most exclusive of such islands. Bedarra had been a secret hideaway of such notable persons as Sarah, Duchess of York and the late Diana, Princess of Wales. While we stayed there we had the interesting experience of meeting Paul McCartney's manager who put me in touch with the famed ex-Beatle who has been responsible for some of the most uplifting musical melodies of the second half of the twentieth century. It is all the more remarkable that McCartney has achieved this without formal musical training. Through Paul McCartney's manager, we exchanged CD's and I was pleased to receive a signed copy of McCartney's *Liverpool Oratorio*. So much of the Beatles' music inspired by McCartney has found expression in lasting instrumental arrangements that are an expression of the hopes that we all felt in those heady days of the 1960's, but Paul continues to compose and his sensitivity comes through like a spiritual message.

Bedarra Island was also a continuation of our rain forest experiences. Much of the small island is covered in rain forest bush. During our stay it lived up to its name. It poured with rain most of the time, but it was a warm tropical rain. There was however, a mystical beauty about that tropical rain especially when we swam in the warm ocean as the squalls beat down all around us. Bedarra is a place for private time.

Our flight from Queensland to Melbourne was not uneventful. At the check-in point we were informed that each of our suitcases must not weigh more than thirty-two pounds. On a four-month concert tour this is an impossibility, especially as most air connections that I had to make are international and not concerned with weight, but rather with quantity of baggage. Here in Australia, however, it was the reverse. We knelt on the floor taking junk out of our suitcases. Books, shoes, clothes, and stuff were jammed into spare plastic bags until finally the weight of each bag passed muster. We now had twice as many pieces of baggage as when we started. At the gate, as always, my flute bag caused further problems. It was considered too big for hand luggage even though it is a regulation size. "What's in there?" the airline official asked.

"My flutes," I responded innocently.

"What kind of fruits?" the man asked mockingly. "Bananas?"

"No, flutes!" I repeated a little more forcefully.

The next thing I knew was that I had to take them all out, open the cases and even play some of them to prove my point.

Finally my flute family and I were permitted to pass through the gate and Peter and I settled on the airplane with a sigh of relief.

After one night in Melbourne, my agent picked us up to join the *Rotterdam*. My show was scheduled for the worst night, the one and only night after a full day in port. On such days, the audience is tired and usually falls asleep. It is no wonder. They would have just been through fourteen hours of four-wheel-drive tours in Australia at 108 degrees! But, I had four days at sea before my concert, so I decided not to worry. Maybe the schedule would change. In the meantime, I enjoyed the lecture program on the ship.

First, there was Art Linkletter, TV personality and host of the shows, *People are Funny* and *Children Say the Darndest Things*. He had the ability to make us laugh at ourselves, which is the first step to releasing the tensions that we hold. Then, I got to hear Charlie Inlander, who lectured on the health system and how to be more informed so that one can sometimes say "No!" to doctors. The following day, Bonnie Pruden showed us how to get rid of pain through trigger points. It is so interesting how self-awareness is now changing the face of medical practice, another indication of the great paradigm shift through which we are all going at the present time.

We also heard from an Aborigine called "Gary" or "Bilgamore," which means "Gentle Crocodile." He said he was visiting from the

Kukuyalanji Aboriginal tribe of Northern Australia and that he normally lived in the rain forest.

What greater contrast could there be in the Queens Lounge of the *Rotterdam* than to have the painted Bilgamore sit there almost totally naked in front of a packed house of wealthy Americans? They watched him warily, rather like they would a rare animal. Then, after his lecture they clamored to have photos taken with him to bring home to their relatives, friends and grandchildren. One can imagine the scene in a suburban living room when the photos were developed—"And look Johnny, this is when we met the wild man from Borneo," only he wasn't from Borneo, but from the related great neighboring island of Australia.

Bilgamore's body was covered with ocher, which is the Aboriginal war paint. He wore only a leather loincloth. I wondered what a more formal Aboriginal outfit might look like? He talked freely about his upbringing in the Aborigine way of living in harmony with nature. He also spoke of "Dream Time."

"Dream Time" has a beginning, but no foreseeable end. Forty thousand years before the first Europeans landed on Australian shores, Aborigines occupied the land. At the time of the first European landings, an estimated 300,000 Aborigines speaking over 500 different languages were spread across the continent in clan groups of 10 to 50 people. Most were hunters or fishermen, but all Aborigines shared a common belief that there was a time back before human reckoning, when everything was first created. This time they call "Dream Time."

Bilgamore informed us of 'Legends' that have been passed down orally from generation to generation explaining the mysteries of how the natural environment was shaped and what role we humans have within this world. "Dream Time" is as much alive today among the aboriginal people as it was in the ancient past. "We consider ourselves as part of nature, sharing a common life-force with everything in the world," Bilgamore explained. "The humans are not above or removed from life, but connected in its very essence."

'How right you are,' I thought to myself.

I could easily be an Aborigine when it comes to their philosophy. Most of the destructive environmental disasters in the last millennia have indeed come about through man's arrogant assumption that we are above all other life forms. Thus we have disturbed the balance of life on this planet.

The passengers were encouraged to ask questions.

"What do you do with your dead people?" one white-haired gentleman asked.

"We sometimes burn them and other times we bury them," Bilgamore answered. "Many still know the art of dying when they feel their time has come. They go, sit and meditate underneath a tree, and then they just die fully prepared." Perhaps this was a little too close to home for the white-haired octogenarian, and so Bilgamore softened his answer with a little Aborigine philosophy.

"We believe the soul of a person never dies, but is transformed into other humans, animals, plants, or even the very rocks and soils around them," Bilgamore explained. "That is why we respect and honor all life forms. You see, I grew up with all this, but then I also went to a regular Australian school. I got to know about videos, discos, alcohol, drugs, and so on. Then one day I just couldn't recognize myself any more. I stopped and decided to change my life. I returned to my origins. So, now I am trying to educate others about our people." He grinned, "Look, I'm not doing too badly. I'm cruising!"

"Is it true that an Aborigine can have more than one wife, perhaps even up to twelve?" a disapproving matron asked.

"Yes, it still happens," Bilgamore replied.

"Could you manage twelve wives?" some eighty-five year old gentleman asked, probably fantasizing.

"No, I couldn't," Bilgamore answered, "I wouldn't have the energy! Besides, it's against the Queen's law, which I respect as the law of Australia."

The discussion then degenerated into legal codes and other mundane matters of Australian society far removed from the essential philosophy of interconnectedness that the aborigines have and still can contribute to our world.

After the questions had died down, Bilgamore gave us a wonderful demonstration of how to play the didgeridoo. He was able to imitate kangaroos, the kookaburra bird, and made Aboriginal war calls on one. The didgeridoo is somewhat like a flute—a long, large pipe that is placed on the ground and held between the feet when being played. It requires a special breathing technique called circular breathing in which one breathes in and out at the same time.

Later, in the evening, I met Gary again at the Midnight buffet. I prefer to call him Gary now, because at the buffet I hardly recognized him. He was wearing jeans and a leather jacket and looked more like a disco fan than an inhabitant of the rain forest. We talked about music and different flutes. There are certain similarities of technique in performance between flutes and the didgeridoo. One is that technique of circular breathing which can greatly enhance a flutist's control and is essential to the didgeridoo. I asked him if he had access to a CD player, as I wanted to give him one of my CD's.

"Yes, I've got one at my home," he assured me.

I smiled. As I looked at the leather jacket and fading blue jeans, I was no longer convinced that Gary lived in the rain forest. Bilgamore might... but Gary...? Maybe Gary's gone "Hollywood" too—but again, we all have a piece of life's puzzle to share.

Perth was our next port, and when in these Australian cities I like to go out to the wildlife parks or zoos and play for the animals. I have given many concerts this way for kangaroos, wallabies, wombats, emus and even Tasmanian devils. My favorites, however, have always been the koalas. On one recent occasion when I played my piccolo for a koala, the cuddly-looking marsupial reached out with its three-fingered paw and grabbed the instrument. He wouldn't let go and sadly wounded my piccolo with his great strength. It wouldn't play. Fortunately, however, I have a remarkable friend in Minneapolis who mends my wounded flutes.

Hans Peterson was recommended to me by a friend as one of the best flute doctors in the country. But, not only was he recommended as one of the best flute doctors, he also lived not too far from me in Minneapolis. When I first met Hans I immediately liked him. He had great warmth and so much humility. We started to talk about facets of each other's lives. He told me about his wife Minnie and asked if I could come and visit sometime. Minnie had been blind for about twenty years and she was in a wheelchair from the first time that I visited them. Every time that I came to their small house in South Minneapolis it was a celebration of love and friendship. Minnie was one of the most loving people I have ever met. She was very frail physically, but extremely strong in spirit. She had a way of calling people over the telephone at precisely the right time. She seemed to have a sixth sense of their troubles or plights. Her timing was always right, and she was there to reconfirm friendship or say some loving words that uplifted the soul. That is so rare. Most people who call us these days want something from us, but Minnie just called to reconfirm the interconnected love of soul. She never complained although she must have been in pain a lot of the time. She never said anything about her condition. She always asked others how they were, but said nothing about herself.

I brought Hans a sick flute and visited with Minnie shortly before she died. It was just after I had become engaged to Peter. I celebrated an early Thanksgiving meal with them and they were so happy about my news. When I left that day, I don't know why, but I hugged Minnie for a long time and heard myself say to her from within, 'Don't be afraid because you are soul and you are carried by divine love... you are love.' Shortly after that I left on a three-month tour.

When I came back to Minneapolis, Hans called me and said Minnie had been in the hospital and was in intensive care. I asked if I could visit the next day, but Hans called the next morning to tell me Minnie had died in the night. At first I felt great sadness that I hadn't gone immediately to see her, but somehow I felt her presence and heard her say to me, "Don't worry... Don't worry... I'm fine. Just keep on playing the music."

Hans asked me to play at the memorial service for Minnie and I was astounded by the crowd gathered, many of whom I had the opportunity to meet. All of them had their own stories of how Minnie had touched their lives. She had this way of reaching out to people and just giving them love. She could not see with her physical eyes, but I believe because of that she was not as distracted and therefore, she could see more with the eyes of soul and the eyes of the heart and maybe she saw more. Realizing how many people Minnie had touched, I reflected on the words of the conducting Minister at the service who said, "Minnie is now in heaven because she believed that Jesus forgave her her sins... that Jesus saved her." I had my own thoughts.... 'She lived and she lives in the heavenly state because she lived in a state of divine love, and to me she is a human saint because she practiced being love, and being an instrument, and being there for others who were in need.' These simple words also came to my mind: "From all the gifts we have to give, the greatest one is how we live." Minnie really did that.

Hans Peterson continues to be the guardian angel of my flute family, and although he had the gift to repair the damage inflicted on a piccolo by an overenthusiastic koala in Australia, his greatest gift to me was the love that he and Minnie shared with me.

The four days between Perth and Bali were filled with interesting lectures to prepare us for the wonders and the mystique of Indonesia. For me, the most interesting lecturer was Dr. Lawrence Blair, an outstanding speaker and also the writer and co-producer with his deceased brother of the TV series *Ring of Fire*. In three brilliant talks he attempted to get across to all of us that we were now entering a very different country.

Indonesia consists of hundreds of islands, including some of the largest in the world: Java, Sumatra, and Borneo. Lawrence Blair referred to the Indonesians as the Oceanic people. They have quite different characteristics from Continental people, the latter being more left-brained. In Indonesia, magic, mysticism and spiritualism are very much alive. Although Islam is the dominant religion, one finds also a lot of Hindus especially on his home island of Bali.

Underlying all religion in Indonesia, and for that matter deep down throughout Asia, is an animism that acknowledges that a Divine force gives life to everything, even so called dead objects. "A truly religious people is one that is tolerant of all religions," noted Lawrence Blair. "In this sense Indonesia is more advanced than the West." But, something that struck me about Dr. Blair's comment on animism was their close resemblance to what we had learned from the Aborigines.

I was sitting right next to the Protestant minister on board the *Rotterdam* and could feel him cringe. The Christian missionaries have managed to disturb almost every native culture by trying to force their beliefs of the "only way," or the "true way," on others. Personally, I find most of them disrespectful of the fact that everyone must have freedom to choose their own religion. After all, the same thing happened to the Native Americans, another culture that embraced this interconnected divine relationship of all life. It makes me sad at times to think of this abuse. How much we could have learned from these people, who quite often knew much more about the "Source of all Life" than many so-called missionaries.

The next morning I had two church "gigs,"—fifteen minutes of solo playing for the Protestants and then ten minutes for communion at the Roman Catholic Mass. I am frequently asked to play for the different religious services on board ships. If Buddhist or Hindu services were offered, I'd play for them on my Tibetan flute as well. Even the clergy appreciate a touch of "Hollywood" magic... a performance to lift the audience out of their internal worries or doldrums.

The Protestants all thought I was a faithful Lutheran and the minister's wife invited me for tea. As we were chatting away, she found out about my near-death experience and invited me to share my experience and thoughts with their Bible-study group the next morning.

'Oh, brother!' I thought to myself, 'Now I'm really getting into trouble.'

The next morning, about seventy Bible-students and the minister assembled in the ship's piano bar. The minister asked me to get up in front of everybody and tell them about my accident of thirty years ago.

The night before, I had thought back in time to the event that had so dramatically changed my life. I recalled again the scene. It had rained heavily that day and the streets were covered with a film of oil and water. My boyfriend's small MG went out of control, ran off the road and smashed into that tree. The only thing I could remember later, was when I woke up in the hospital and knew that I had seen the car, with us in it, from way up above... sort of from a soul or spiritual perspective. At that time, I was aware of a totally different state, closer to a peaceful floating. There was no pain. A light engulfed me and some wonderful sounds came with the light. There was a feeling of total acceptance even when I was parted from my boyfriend Joern by that glass-like wall. I also remembered seeing my body in the car and giving the police, who had finally arrived, some sort of information about our address. Then, suddenly, after what seemed a totally timeless period, I awoke in that hospital room. I was disoriented and had no idea what had happened. But, somewhere deep inside I knew that my boyfriend had not come back to Earth with me.

It took some time to heal the pain of that loss. But, I absolutely knew from then on that we are neither our bodies nor our minds. There is no death of the soul. That Divine energy which drives the body and mind, our soul, is our real self. At the moment of death it just leaves this life behind like an old coat. Some call it soul, some call it the spirit or the individual consciousness. It really doesn't matter what one calls it, any more than it matters what you call God—it's essence. Yet, every one can experience themselves as soul. Living in a mindful awareness of ourselves as spiritual beings should be the most powerful, life-giving way to spend each moment, as it was for my friend Minnie. Just pay attention to the moment and it's spiritual opportunity, this is the best way to enrich life. All this I instinctively knew when I returned from death. Now, standing in front of all these Bible students I was trying to find the words to describe an experience for which words seem so inadequate.

"Thank you so much for inviting me here today to share my near-death experience with you," I started to say, while they all stared at me with very serious expressions. "First of all I'd like to mention that many people have had an experience similar to mine. There are at least eight-and-a-half million Americans who have had a near-death or out-of-body experience. These days you can find many books and even talk shows that discuss it openly." Then I proceeded to describe the accident and my "Spiritual Awakening." I revealed my first contact with divine "Light and Sound," and how it started me on a spiritual search for my internal truth. "What I found in these last thirty years of life is the simple truth that each and every living being is a spark of God," I explained to these devoted Christians. "Everyone is on that same journey to recognize our origins. And this is really all we have to do: 'Remember who we are, in the moment.' We are soul, the essence of the source... God returning to God. When we remember our essence as we go about our daily experiences in life, we can then be conscious co-workers with our internal God force! Intention is all. Intend to let God's love flow through you and it will. It's that simple."

Some nodded in agreement; others in my audience nervously clutched their Bibles giving occasional glances in the direction of the Minister or Pastor.

"Now that it is many years after my accident, I have simplified my quest for spiritual truth," I continued. "Now, I just spend a few minutes each day on some simple spiritual exercises. It might be just breathing and meditating, or thinking of something I'm grateful for, that opens my heart to the light and sound of God in each moment. There are many ways to do this. Prayer is a good way," I suggested in the hope that this might be more acceptable to this particular group. Prayer, after all, does focus intent. "So is visualization, chanting, singing, or even exercising. It doesn't matter what your practice is as long as you intend to clear the heart and mind to serve God and express that happiness. I believe a happy life is the greatest gift we can give God, ourselves, and others."

The main ingredient of this talk was simple: sincerity of the heart. I didn't expect to change anyone's mind. God's presence is always with us, because we are part of God. We cannot escape this.

The Bible class students looked at me with a mixture of skepticism and curiosity. Then the minister asked if anyone else had had a similar experience. About four people raised their hands.

One lady came up to the front with me and said she left her body while giving birth to her second child. She described how she went through a tunnel towards a great light and stayed in this peaceful place till the doctors suddenly brought her back. "I never knew what that was, and I have been embarrassed to talk about it," she said. "But, now with all these books coming out, I recognize it as a near-death experience. It always stayed with me as a very special moment."

Another woman from the class raised her hand and addressed the lady who had just shared her experience. "Don't you know that most people hallucinate while under anesthesia? That's what happened to you! You were just hallucinating!"

The woman who had bravely spoken out looked at me for encouragement. I could feel and see her heart drop. She smiled weakly and quietly sat down. I met her afterwards to talk with her and share with her how real these experiences are, and yet how hard it is to relate them to others who have never had them.

The minister now felt it was time to get on with the Bible study and read the day's quote. They all discussed it. I had to stay for the whole thing, but I really didn't mind. Actually, I found it quite interesting even though I had to bite my tongue from time to time.

Afterward, another woman cornered me. She was somehow convinced that I had been misled. She told me how much more reliable and real the Bible was than any human experience. "The Bible is the word of God," she exclaimed, pounding her copy of the book with her right hand. "Jesus said that we all have wicked hearts and that the only way we can be saved from our own wickedness is through him giving us a new heart."

'My God,' I thought to myself, 'what a strange thing to hang over people's heads and what a grave misunderstanding of God. Look at a newborn child. Do you see a wicked heart? And besides that, the New Testament of the Bible certainly was not written until thirty to eighty years after Jesus of Nazareth walked this earth. Who really knows what Jesus said.' I was reminded of my husband Peter Longley's books—*Two Thousand Years Later* and *The Magdala Trilogy*. For me, they contain a much deeper and more meaningful message of Jesus. But, I said nothing. 'Why is it is so much harder for people to trust and acknowledge their own spirituality,' I thought, 'than to follow the hide-bound rules and beliefs of "religion?" Why do so many rather put their trust in a collection of books called the Bible?'

Then the minister asked the question I had been asked so many times: "But you do believe in Jesus Christ, don't you? You do believe he died for our sins and that he is the Son of God, don't you?"

I paused for a moment, as they were now all looking at me again with intense expectation. I didn't want to shock them, but I had to be honest and stand up for my reality. "Yes, I do honor and respect Jesus," I said. "And yes, I do believe he was the son of God, but no more and no less than you and I are! We all come from the same source and we all are sons and daughters of God... the difference lies in the degree of realization of our God nature."

After that revelation, the fundamentalist woman tried even harder to convince me that I can only be saved through Jesus. She didn't really hear me when I mentioned that I didn't think that anybody had to be saved, as we are already divine soul.

Finally, I had to go. I thanked everybody for letting me share my near-death experience. 'People believe what they want to believe,' I thought to myself. 'But, that is precisely why no belief system can contain the real truth. It is best to leave it at that.'

When people ask me about these things so directly, I have to tell them that not everyone can believe only the stories written in the Bible. Maybe the time has come when more people will be nudged by Spirit through their real experiences... their own experiences of God. Soul lives in the moment. What we are experiencing now is surely our best spiritual truth! We are forging our own spiritual lessons, which add to all our understanding of love and God. Enjoy the moment... the now, that is my religion. Whether performing in "Hollywood" like my actor friend or Art Linkletter, or lecturing on a cruise ship like Lawrence Blair, or in your everyday life like Minnie Peterson, it still applies.

# Chapter Sixteen

# *South East Asia*

S outh East Asia is my favorite part of the world. I love the lush landscape, the lithe gentle people, the ethnic food and the expectation for the future, for Asia is the probable future of our world. This had first dawned on me when I lived in China for that brief spell in the 1980's. Singapore is the miracle city of Asia and was founded by Sir Stamford Raffles in 1819 to be "a crossroads of Asian culture and trade." Singapore today is truly just that.

Arriving in Singapore, I am always struck by the city's pristine facade and efficiency. Everything works like clockwork—streets are washed frequently, buses and trams run on time, white-gloved policemen direct orderly lines of cars. It is a pleasant place to visit for a few days, but there is another side to this veneer. Everything and everyone is strictly regulated. Spitting gum on the street can land you in jail. The city is free of chaos and traffic jams, and there is not the usual pollution, dirt and smell that emanates from most Asian cities. But, at what price, I wonder?

Singapore is modern and very busy. If residents are not standing at a street corner with one ear to their cellular phone, and there are more cellular phones per capita in Singapore than in any other country in the world, people seem to be running and hurrying all the time. This makes for vibrancy, but in reality people are so busy because they often work several jobs to afford the very high cost of living. Of course the rat race continues in many western countries as well. We are quite good at it in the United States and Europe, but for some reason it is not expected in Singapore, which historically we still associate with the leisurely colonial world of Somerset Maugham and Noel Coward. You can still sip gin slings in the Long Bar at *Raffles* hotel, but at a price! In reality, Maugham and Coward would barely recognize the modern metropolis and enormous container port that is Singapore today.

Some time ago I heard a saying, which always comes back to me when I start running, rushing and hurrying: "The problem with the rat race is, that even if you win it, you are still a rat."

But, where in this world is the perfect balance between efficiency, dynamics, success, and peace, not to mention relaxation? Probably that balance can only be achieved within the individual.

I have made many visits to Singapore. On this occasion, because of terrorist bombings in Israel my flight from Singapore to Haifa was canceled. I didn't know where my agent was going to send me, but he wanted me to pick up another ship in the Mediterranean. I really didn't worry about it too much; by this time I had learned that travel plans usually come together in time, and that changes are very often a door to new adventures.

During this interim in Singapore, I performed a concert and gave a lecture on "Dreams" which brought a crowd who responded vividly to my music. They also laughed at the stories I told, and they especially enjoyed our stuffed bear named Caramel. My husband Peter called him Caramel Bear because of his color. The bear gave a speech about love toward the end of the program.

Once again, stuffed animals show up as being important in my life. I had a huge brown bear as a little girl who was a very close friend before my pony arrived. He was worn out from hugging and squeezing. Later, at the time of my divorce, a bear brought comfort. But, then at age forty-three, thanks to Peter, many new bears came into my life. When I met my second husband, I discovered that he had about thirty stuffed pandas!

My first husband, Harold, was not much into stuffed animals, but he was responsible for bringing Dr. Crow into my life. He won the crow, or close relative of Heckel and Jekyl, at a fair in Reno. We brought the toy home and there she sat on a window shelf until Peter came into my life. Peter breathed life into the stuffed bird, and it sat by his computer for many days while Peter was writing *Two Thousand Years*

*Later*. One day, in jest, Peter put a pair of glasses on the crow, which made her look very learned. He then decided that because of the black bird's excellent advice and editorial work on the book, she should be awarded a doctorate when and if Peter got the book published. The book was published in December 1996, and from then on Harold Ware's crow became our Dr. Crow. I have never quite agreed with Peter about the gender of this friendly, if somewhat earnest bird; I personally consider the crow to be a female, but he insists that she is male. How do you tell with a bird? Anyway, a surprise came for Harold Ware when he got married again. The crow, whom he had ignored all those years, but in all fairness whom he had won, attended his wedding. Peter arranged the flowers for the ceremony and I played flute with a string quartet that I had organized for Harold. It was a wonderful wedding, Harold marrying a tall, slender and beautiful young bride, and I was so glad that he had found the same happiness as I have. Peter had placed Dr. Crow at the foot of the altar. The stuffed bird was the first thing Harold saw when he walked up the aisle.

Today, Peter and I have about sixty stuffed animals of all colors and races, but mostly bears. At least five accompany us at all times. These world travelers provide lots of laughter. They talk of course, and break down any barriers with others. Now, here in Singapore, the fluffy Caramel Bear addressed my audience:

"We bears are very glad to come to you," Caramel said as I brought him out from under the table to happy laughter. "We have a very important message to give to all of you: 'Love is the only real thing in life.' We are here to provide this for people of all ages. Remember that we bears are always close to you and we might even appear in your dreams. Sometimes, my bear spirit has come into my own dreams revealing my past life as a polar bear and on one occasion as a panda."

Caramel Bear with his words of wisdom received the loudest applause of the evening.

Dreams are actually very important to me. I have always kept a dream journal, because I have learned a lot from my dreams. I have dreamed many insights and creative solutions that have been fulfilled in my life. So, I always try to find a way to encourage my audience to listen to their dreams. Remember, my marriage to Peter was predicted in a dream!

Through Caramel Bear, I had reminded this audience to let in the love that is always there. It didn't matter to me if his appearance seemed a little corny, because the life-energy always perks up a lot when a bear comes out. Humor makes it much easier to relate to people.

One of the passengers from the Greek ship on which I had just been performing was staying several days in Singapore before flying home to the United States. She was a lovely older lady with a very adventuresome spirit and a great sense of humor. At eighty years old, she was still hungry for experience and knowledge.

When I joined the ship in Bali I had asked her about a cast on her arm, she said: "Two weeks ago I was dancing with the Greek waiters in the dining room. I fell and broke it! It had to be put in a cast at a Malaysian hospital." It did not in any way dampen her spirit. "At least I broke it while I was having fun," she explained.

We became good friends on our voyage to Singapore through South East Asia. I promised I would call on her while we were both in Singapore, although we were staying at different hotels. "Hi Muriel," I said on the phone, "Have you been dancing with any waiters recently?"

"Is that you Bettine?", she shouted, "What a joy to hear your voice. No, I haven't danced, but guess what I did last night?"

"What?" I exclaimed.

"I went on a night safari at the zoo and visited with all the wild animals like the cougars, tigers and lions. Tomorrow I will have breakfast with an orangutan."

"Oh my! Muriel, you're impossible!" I replied, my sympathy turning to envy. "I just wanted to ask you if you would like to go out to eat with us tonight?"

"I'd love to. Can you come up and fetch me?" the game old lady replied.

"I'll be there at seven," I suggested and hung up.

It took some time to get Muriel organized and into the restaurant. Over a Chinese meal she met four of my Singapore friends, a young couple whom I've known a long time and a Tai Chi Master and his wife. We all enjoyed each other's company. All of a sudden Muriel turned white. "Can you help me to the ladies' room?" she asked as politely as she could. Leaning on me, she confessed, "I feel so awful. I'm nauseous and weak".

In the restroom, she almost collapsed, but after resting a moment she started to feel a little better and said she wanted to go back to the table. On the way back, the nausea started all over again. "Would you say the Lord's Prayer with me?" she asked in a whisper.

'I sure hope she isn't going to die right here,' I thought before politely answering, "Sure Muriel." But, I wasn't certain of the words in English although I could recite the Lord's Prayer from childhood Lutheran memory in German.

We said the Lord's Prayer right there in the hall, she in English and I in German. Something magical happened. Energy flowed into both of us, and she went on with the evening. The Tai Chi Master put his arm around her to give her support and energy. But, when we helped her back into the car, she fainted. I was fearful, as her condition despite the temporary improvement, now looked really serious.

"Shall we bring her to the emergency room?" my friends suggested.

"Yes, I think so," I replied.

"I can't see anymore," Muriel whispered as we held comforting hands in the taxi. I spontaneously started singing that ancient name for God, which I chant daily in contemplation—"Hu." The others joined in and the air filled with a choir of voices. We all chanted really loudly and with lots of love.

Gradually, Muriel relaxed and her breathing returned to normal. "I can see again," she revealed. "Please don't bring me to the hospital; I'm much better now. What was that beautiful sound? I felt so much better when I heard it."

"That's just a way of connecting with God," I said. "For me it brings in the divine love, the light and sound of God's energy. Sound can be very healing."

When I got her to bed, she asked if I could chant that sound again. She fell asleep to the hum of "Hu." Such chanting has been used by Tibetan monks and various Indian religious groups, and by Christian monks in the West, for generations. Some sing "Om," and others "Nam" or Latin words. Any chant that produces a certain vibration can have a healing effect raising one's personal life force.

Muriel was much better the next morning when I called. Happily, she informed me: "By the way, Bettine, I have found out that we can have tea with the orangutans at the zoo, so if I keep improving at this rate I might go."

'Doesn't she ever slow down?' I wondered to myself. But, I knew it was no good talking someone out of something they really wanted to do, even if it was a questionable project. I saw her one more time and she had indeed canceled her visit to the orangutans. She needed to return home and rest from her adventures, but she had gained enough strength for her to travel.

Eventually a ticket arrived by courier from my agent. I had only about three hours before my flight, which was apparently to Cyprus. This was fine with me. I had never been to Cyprus. I just made it to Singapore's amazing airport on time. During the fourteen hours on the British Airways flight I had a little time to digest my Singapore experiences and all those delicious Chinese meals. I had to admire Muriel's spirit. The song of her life was obviously almost at an end, but she had never stopped singing.

Singaporeans are the most Westernized of the South East Asian peoples in as much as their economy is the most buoyant and their standard of living the highest, but the Thais and Vietnamese seem more gentle people. I have been particularly impressed with Vietnam on my several visits to that tragic, but incredibly beautiful country. The first time, the ship I was on made a call at Natrang.

Standing on deck as we anchored just outside a small harbor filled with colorful boats that were a cross between Chinese junks and sampans, I wondered what sort of a reception a shipload of Americans would receive in Vietnam. Images of the terrible ten-year war that had flashed across our TV sets nightly during the 1960's and early 1970's came unbidden into my mind. This was probably one of the most senseless wars in history, undoubtedly prolonged by the American wish to bolster a friendly but corrupt Western style government in Saigon in a struggle against the communist and nationalist aspirations of the leader of the north, Ho Chi Minh. American might showed its muscle and not only prolonged this war, but wrought unbelievable ecological destruction to one of the most beautiful countries in the world. Although Ho Chi Minh died before the fall of Saigon, his dream was realized. The Americans failed to contain his guerrilla forces and in the aftermath of failure and through enormous political pressure from the grass roots at home, pulled out of a venture that it would probably have been better for the world if they had never got into. But, the thinking of the late 1950's and the early 1960's in the aftermath of the collapse of mainland China to communism and the Korean war's attempt to contain it, was in the hands of those who had won World War II in the struggle with Japan, and they believed they were invincible and that they could police the world. There were genuine concerns that Malaya and Indonesia would fall to communism if a stand was not made in Vietnam, and it is possible that without the Vietnam War this might indeed have happened. Today, the Western nations might say 'Would it have mattered?' But, then, it seemed to matter a lot. A whole generation was still alive that had fought World War II on principles of personal freedom. Communism did not represent to the West personal freedom, and when one considers the atrocities of Stalin in Russia and Chairman Mao in China, one can understand why.

Vietnam today is a communist country. Although as a nation it has a long way to go to raise its standard of living, I have been convinced on my visits that the people have hearts that are free!

Stepping ashore in Natrang, I was well aware that a million Vietnamese people had been killed in the Vietnam War. I was also well aware of the senseless loss of life that Americans, Australians, New Zealanders and others involved had incurred, but by far the greatest loss of life was Vietnamese. As soon as I walked out into the unmade streets of the harbor area, however, and saw those smiling Vietnamese faces I knew that this was now a facet of this turbulent land's history. A gentleness captured my heart immediately. There was no animosity or bitterness in the faces of these lovely people. Even the many beggars lacked aggression.

Two young men approached my husband and me with broad open smiles. They offered to bring us to a beach on their motorcycles. We hopped on to their Hondas and held on tight. Off we went through the crowded streets of Natrang toward the long sandy beaches. When they dropped us off at a local restaurant on the ocean, I asked them about their families. They had no family. Their parents had all been killed in the Vietnam War.

It was indescribably beautiful on that local beach. Distant mountains gave a backdrop of vibrant colors. The air was filled with an invigorating energy. But, it was the gentle nature of the people with their childlike and unspoiled smiles that left the greatest impression.

We enjoyed a wonderful Vietnamese lunch of spring rolls and fish. While we were eating, one of the waitresses shyly walked by and smiled. I smiled back at her and commented on the great food. "I learning English," she announced with a sweet expression. Pretty soon we were in conversation about her country and our travels around the world. Before we left, I gave her a cassette tape of my music hoping that she could find a player. She was so grateful and in that gratitude I felt I sensed her soul. I felt humbled in her presence.

It has become so rare to casually experience pure and innocent qualities in people. But, in Vietnam one can still find them. I closed my eyes several times on our speedy ride back to the harbor area on those motor bikes. The Vietnamese are not used to cars and among the sea of bicycles the motor bike is king. Why look when faced with such terror on the road? Instead, I gazed internally at the simple goodness in the face of my new friend. It stayed with me and sank into my heart forever. Occasionally, she writes to me. Recently, three years after we met at that restaurant, she sent me a photograph of herself.

Back at the harbor village, we explored the narrow streets. There was colorful poverty here. There was a continuous line of children and young women carrying water in a vast range of containers from the one and only village well. Pigs and chickens roamed as freely in the mud-rutted streets as people did. There were few shops to sell tourist T shirts, but there was a strong sense of family life. Perhaps because families had suffered so much in the previous generation, they now felt bound in love. In front of hovel homes each family group would sit wearing conical hats to protect them from the sun. They smiled, they waved and they welcomed. The past has been forgotten and they have forgiven.

On that first visit to Vietnam, we also stopped at Vung Tau, the port city on a rugged peninsula that sits near the mouth of the Saigon river in the Mekong delta. This town had been fashionable in the French colonial period. Here at the White Palace the last of the Vietnamese Emperors had held court under French surveillance and here in the earlier part of this century, colonial administrators from Saigon had built homes at this resort. Trappings of that former elegance can still be seen, but it is best expressed in the Vietnamese women whose lithe beauty is enhanced by the graceful "au dzai" that they wear flapping in the wind as they sit bolt upright on their motor cycles.

A bus took us from the ship, which was docked a long way from the town. At the place where we were dropped off there were a few tourist stalls selling lacquered wood work and shell paintings along with that first batch of tourist clothing—Vietnamese T shirts. Some passengers did not venture beyond this small market, but there were a number of willing men in stiff conical hats who were prepared to pedal us around the peninsula, a considerable ride in a pedicab, for a paltry sum. We accepted.

Being pedaled through a Vietnamese town is a strange experience. The streets are very crowded, but surprisingly silent because of the few motorized vehicles. It was almost like riding through a snowstorm as hundreds of bicycles passed us in both directions. The only sound was the ringing of their bells and the occasional sound of phlegm being spat out by our pedaling driver. It is amazing how even in three years, however, motorized traffic has increased. More recently I was driven by pedicabs through the streets of Hanoi and Ho Chi Minh City. It was a more frightening experience than that first graceful ride through Vung Tau. Traffic comes at you from all directions. There seems to be no rule of the road. In a pedicab one sits in front of the cyclist and rather low toward the ground; in a collision there would be no protection.

I had set my mind on going into Hanoi from Haiphong by myself, either by taxi, motorbike or train. Hanoi was three hours away. I started early in the morning, walking briskly through the Haiphong harbor towards the gates that led into the town. I had Bacpac Bear with me and a small carry-on suitcase holding just enough for a one night stay in Hanoi. As I walked through the gates I was startled by one of the guards yelling at me: "Stop!"

I obeyed, and then walked over to him and pulled out my various papers along with my crew card and my visa for Vietnam, feeling secure that all of my documents were in order. The guard looked at them and then asked: "Where you go?"

"Hanoi", I responded.

"No!" he shouted.

"But I have all the right papers to go!" I protested.

"No!" he yelled again.

It became obvious that he did not understand any English, so I tried in French. No success! Only the forceful: "No!" came back to me. Now, as a last resort, Bacpac chimed in with humor. My backpack bear started to talk to the guard in that broken pidgin English so many humans also use when they are faced with foreign language barriers: "We go Hanoi! We okay with papers!"

"No!" the guard said firmer than ever.

I made Bacpac shiver in fright, but that got no response from the rigid official. I felt this funny anxiety in the pit of my stomach that I remember from schooldays when the teachers would reprimand me.

"Passport!" the official yelled.

"Passport on ship!" I shouted back, getting a bit desperate. As crewmembers we always have to leave our passports on the ship. " I go to Hanoi now!" I said very assertively.

"No!" the official screamed.

This was too much. I gave in. I turned around and ran back to the ship. By now it was already 10:00 a.m. and I could feel the heat of the sun burning down on my Vietnamese conical hat and the sweat pouring from my hairline. I sped up the gangway and went straight to the Purser's Office, where I explained the situation.

"No problem!" the female purser said. "Here is your passport! But, be careful and don't miss the ship tomorrow!"

Triumphantly, I ran back down the gangway, feeling confident that I would make it to Hanoi after all. At the foot of the gangway I saw a limousine and two men waiting. They approached me and one of them announced in broken English: "We told to bring lady Hanoi. You lady?"

I was startled. How could that have been arranged so fast? "I don't think so..." I stammered, assuming that this service must have been arranged for some wealthy passenger.

"Yes. You lady," the driver insisted as he pointed at Bacpac Bear. "You lady with bear."

I put two and two together and realized that the guard at the gate must have arranged this. Now, I had to ask the price! "How much?" I questioned.

"One hundred twenty dollar," the other man answered.

"No way!" I countered; knowing that this was twice as much as it should cost. "I am a crew member and not a passenger! After several negotiations we finally settled on sixty-five dollars, and Bacpac and I settled into the nice air-conditioned car. When we reached the harbor gate I waved and smiled at the official, who faintly smiled back. Obviously, he had done enough yelling for the day.

The drive to Hanoi was a mixture of beauty and danger. The traffic was horrendous with motor bikes and bicycles coming out of nowhere and the narrow roads being totally overcrowded. But, we also drove by the most beautiful rice fields. It was hard to imagine that here there had been total destruction in the Vietnam war years and that in the midst of this serene landscape so many bombs had wrought such havoc. Finally, we got to Hanoi and the driver let me off at the Metropole hotel—one of the finer hotels in the city. I booked a room, which I got for a huge discount. The Asian financial crisis was also being felt in Vietnam and hotels were very eager to get at least some business. Then, I went out to explore the city.

I took one of those pedicabs, and at first when my driver started out into the middle of the traffic chaos, I simply screamed. Cars, motorbikes and cyclists came right at me from all directions—it was as if my pedicab was under attack! "No worry! You okay!" my driver assured me. Apparently, he was used to these screams from other foreigners.

Hanoi is architecturally splendid with its old French colonial buildings and a lovely lake in its midst. While there, I went to four music stores buying a total of twelve bamboo flutes for one dollar each. But, the beautiful Vietnamese "au Dzai" truly caught my eye and I could not resist purchasing blue and white silk outfits from local venders. Vietnamese women are extremely slender, small-boned and very beautiful. I had to get extra large for my outfits and felt somewhat embarrassed.

In the evening, I saw a wonderful water puppet show with authentic Vietnamese music played masterfully on various ethnic instruments. In the hotel, I also met several reporters from America who had lived in Vietnam for several years, but now planned to move. They shared their experiences and viewpoints on Vietnam with me—"There really are these two sides to Vietnam—there are the very warm, sweet and wonderful people, who are so forgiving and humble, and then, on the other side there is this totally strict and corrupt government which imprisons those people."

The next morning, I had to think about getting back to the ship. I decided to take the train. A pedicab brought me to the train station, which looked more like a chicken farm. There were chickens running all over the forecourt. Again, nobody spoke English or French. I walked up to the ticket window and said: "Haiphong? Train to Haiphong? First class?" A ticket was pushed through the window. I looked at the price. It was the equivalent of five dollars for first class! I remembered the car driver had wanted one hundred and twenty dollars—quite a difference! Settling into the train, I hoped that this was the right one and that it would eventually start moving, because at first we just sat there for about half an hour. Time was marching on and I knew that the ship would not wait for me, and that it would cause trouble if one of the crewmember's passports were not back. Finally, the train started. I believe I was the only Westerner on board and everybody looked at me as they would look at a rare animal in a zoo! I smiled and then they smiled back. No words were needed. But, several times I asked: "Haiphong? Train to Haiphong?" When they all nodded reassuringly, I relaxed and settled back into my seat. The journey was to be four hours. A small Vietnamese man came to serve tea. This was a special service for first class passengers. Then, young girls came by selling candy.

We continued communicating most of the time by just smiling. Then, some officials came through the train. My heart sank, as I feared a repeat of the same scenario as the day before. But, the officials also just smiled when they asked for my ticket. Bacpac Bear was sitting next to me in his usual slumped over position. One of the officials wanted to pick him up. They laughed as the man held him in the air and then hugged him and even kissed him. They were like children and there was no harsh official energy there at all. Encouraged by their joy, I took out a bamboo flute and played. The officials and some of the passengers on the train then got up and danced. We had a concert and a party in the train all at the same time! Bacpac was passed from person to person as they danced just like it had happened in the Alexandrine mosque with the mullahs. When I took out the piccolo, the dancing got even more joyful and wild.

Outside the window there were rice fields. Many Vietnamese workers looked up when the train came past and waved. We all waved back and they laughed and smiled. 'What a great celebration of the spirit of oneness and understanding and love,' I thought. There was just goodwill and playfulness and connectedness among us—no animosity, no prejudice... just people playing like children and enjoying each other!

The time passed so fast. All of a sudden we arrived in Haiphong. I was sad to leave my new found friends with whom I had not spoken a single word, and yet we had felt so close and happy. I gave them some cassettes, some shampoos and lotions along with postcards from the ship—they were overjoyed. Bacpac Bear waved "Good-bye." I looked at my watch; I would even make it back to the ship on time. Another pedicab was at the station to bring me to the harbor, and when I entered that same gate again that had been so troublesome the day before, I could not help myself but have Bacpac wave at that same official and shout: "Hanoi—Wonderful!" The guard seemed to be in a better mood and joyfully waved back! Exhausted and totally happy, I entered the ship grateful for the cool air and the comfort of my cabin and sank into a deep sleep dreaming about friendly open Vietnamese faces.

Our next stop was Ho Chi Minh City, formerly Saigon, where the ship docked right next to the city center. I looked forward to more adventures. This time I chose a motor bike for transportation. I found a friendly driver. I looked him in the eyes and he seemed honest. His energy felt good. So I hopped onto his bike and off we went into the middle of that traffic chaos. His name was Le-Minh and he spoke quite good English. He was about twenty years old and a terrific driver. He always found a way through this labyrinth of cars and bikes! I had asked him to bring me to the Music Conservatory. Soon we arrived at a beautiful old building and I went inside to meet some of the music professors. After some explaining the Vice President of the Conservatory came out to meet me. He was quite a famous violinist, who had studied at the Tschaikovsky Conservatory in Moscow and he spoke English, Russian and Vietnamese. We had a wonderful talk about music and orchestras and I gave him some of my CDs.

"Why don't you come back next year and play a concert for us here?" he suggested.

We said "So long" and I felt the same hospitality and friendship I had felt on my visit to China. Music is such a great bridge between different cultures and people. It cuts right through any prejudices and feelings of separation.

Le-Minh and I sped off into the town again and he showed me many interesting places including the theater and the famous Q-Bar that was and still is a meeting place for many foreigners. Several more flutes and percussion instruments were bought and also a few more "au dzais," which only cost about twenty dollars even if they are custom tailored. Le-Minh also acted as a fashion advisor, giving approval signs each time I walked out into the street modeling another outfit and asking him for his advice. We got along very well, and he was overjoyed about the thirty dollars I gave him for the day. He had been the best guide I could have wished for and I felt I had made a new friend in a totally foreign country. Some of the passengers had seen me zoom by on the bike several times that day, and in the evening when we all stood at the railing to wave "Good-bye" to this friendly, warmhearted country, they expressed their concern.

"I am fine," I told them. "I had the best guide ever and I managed to see so much and he was totally honest and grateful." I felt that I had experienced again that people really often are as we expect them to be. We project something out to them and they give it back. And if they sometimes seem to be not too friendly, as in the case of the official at the gate in Haiphong, then there is always still a way to get around them. "Sempre tem jeito," the Brazilians had taught me, and I keep practicing that around the world.

When ships visit Thailand they are certain to dock within striking distance of Bangkok, the vibrant, but terribly polluted capital of this land of beautiful people. The Thais, like their northern neighbors in Vietnam, have to be among the most exquisite peoples of the world. It is not surprising, therefore, that for ship's crews Thailand is one of the most anticipated ports of call on any world cruise. Ship's usually dock in Liam Chabang overnight to accommodate tours into Bangkok where the incredible architectural treasures of the Royal Palace complex and the colorful floating markets of the klongs await the eager photographer. But, Liam Chabang is much closer to Pattaya, which developed as a rest and recreation center for American troops during the Vietnam War. The girlie bars and licentious night life of Pattaya's "Go-go" strip is what attracts most crewmembers.

The strip is a shadow of what it once was as Thailand has attempted to deal with the dual problems that arose from such development— Aids and teenage prostitution. But, it is still an eye opener for the innocent as the most beautiful girls in the world hook in the men. The prostitution is quite blatant as the bargirls in the scantiest of clothing nestle up to male visitors. The dancers are unashamedly seductive and the night shows raucous. Although some of the best Thai massage can be found in Pattaya, along the strip massage means something else as eager customers pick out their masseuses in large picture windows.

But, apart from massage in its various guises, there is also good economic shopping in Pattaya; an incredible elephant show staged in magnificent orchid gardens; an impressive orphanage of gifted and disabled Thai children run by Father Brennan, and some of the most beautiful hotels in the world.

When I am at Liam Chabang I try to visit my friends in Bangkok. Nita and Suhkbir are members of the Indian community living in the bustling city. They are Sikhs and male Sikhs are forbidden to cut their locks, so Suhkbir always wears a turban over his long hair. They are quite influential in their community and usually arrange for me to perform a concert. At one such concert I was even able to dedicate a piece to the King of Thailand, who is himself a keen jazz musician. There are usually an interesting cross-section of people at these concerts—Thais, many Indians, and some English-speaking guests. On the last occasion, after the concert we all celebrated being together with a wonderful Indian meal. The courses were accompanied by sitar and tabla music until well after midnight.

The next morning brought me back to a woman I met with Nita the previous year. I love Indian dress and although I have many good friends who have advised me on saris and punjabis in Bombay, I have found Nita's outlets in Bangkok to be the most rewarding. We made our way to one of Nita's favorite Indian stores. As the door of the Punjabi shop swung open I immediately recognized the face of the owner. She was the woman I had met the previous year and at that time she had shared with me that her husband was dying of cancer. Her beautiful dark eyes were filled with deep sadness. I realized that her husband must have died. She didn't have to tell me. She recognized me instantly, but then, how many blonde Caucasians does she have coming in to buy real Indian punjabis!

Immediately, we both felt a deep connection. Looking through punjabis together was just an excuse to share our unexplained love and friendship that can only be understood as soul love. I asked my inner self to ease the pain of her grief. However prepared we are, the death of a family member is the hardest and most transforming experience.

We sat down outside and she spoke gently about the isolation she felt from other people at this time. It was hard to respond to her questions about life and death and the purpose of it all. Nita and I just listened and shared our love. Listening is so important, and when we all got up we had tears of compassion in our eyes. I hugged this beautiful and gentle person "Good-bye." I could feel in my heart all the pain she felt, but also at the same time a strange joy and gratitude for meeting her again half way around the world. We had connected so deeply in such a short moment of time. She had reminded me of the preciousness of life.

On that particular visit to Thailand my ship made a second stop at an island in southeast Thailand called Ko Sumi. After the heaviness of that second day in Bangkok, Ko Sumi was a delightful escape. The island is beautiful, lush and surrounded by magnificent white sand beaches. There are a number of exquisite resorts all landscaped with billowing tropical flowers. There are no towns of any size on Ko Sumi and the Thai people here are villagers. Their natural gentleness and grace reflects the peace of their island home.

As I sat looking out at the ocean from one of these palm fringed beaches, I reflected on events in other parts of our world—terrorist attacks, suicide bombings, Bosnia, Africa and the volatile nature of financial markets. The moments of inner peace are so precious and yet outer life is so often in turmoil. But, you can carry your own paradise within you, I decided. I pulled out my Tibetan flute and held it in my hands with loving care before attempting to express my inner peace. 'Perhaps it is not just what you do, but how you do it,' I thought. 'Giving love with each action, however small: surely this is a worthy spiritual gift to offer.'

I played a few notes over the still humid air. Two Thai children appeared from nowhere and watched me, a girl and a boy. Children have a habit of appearing from nowhere. I watched the girl as I played, noting her mature dark eyes. 'You will grow up to be a beauty,' I thought. 'Don't ever leave paradise.'

I started this chapter at Asia's crossroads, Singapore, but I should close by sharing some experiences of Hong Kong, China's window on the world. Many comparisons used to be made between Singapore and Hong Kong. Both centers are Asian clearinghouses, huge outlets for international shoppers and bankers. They are modern cities containing some of the world's most dynamic new architecture. Most important of all, both Hong Kong and Singapore are Chinese cities, the overwhelming majority of their separate populations being racially and culturally Chinese. Singapore and Hong Kong were both bastions of the British Empire, but today they are leading centers of a new Empire—Asia. I believe that Asia, led by China, will be the most significant power of the twenty-first Century both politically and culturally.

There is always a lot of excitement on board a Cruise ship approaching Hong Kong. Almost every passenger is out on deck. High-rise skyscrapers appear mysteriously out of the early-morning haze, the air is invigorating and the atmosphere exciting in this bustling business center. Ahead can be seen one of the world's most magnificent suspension bridges linking Hong Kong's new airport to the mainland of the New Territories and Kowloon. On the right, ships pass Stanley, Repulse Bay and the rocky headland that is home to Ocean World, Hong Kong's theme park that boasts the longest escalator in the world. Rounding Victoria Peak the intense downtown areas of Central, Wan Jai and Kowloon come into view. These are the most familiar areas to many passengers—here are found the shopping malls and the luxury hotels.

For many travelers Hong Kong is only about shopping, which is sad in a way as this great city prepares itself for a dominant role in bridging together the two Asias of Communist China and the intensively capitalist countries that make up much of the rest of Asia. The shopping is almost overwhelming in quantity, but to be truthful, today you can find most items cheaper in America! But, tourists still believe they'll find incredible bargains in Hong Kong. After a ship has docked at the Ocean Terminal the passengers run down the gangway like ants spreading out into a maze of malls. Three-day shopping sprees ensue. They return to the ship totally exhausted. The luggage shops also fare well. Many passengers have to buy extra suitcases just to tote their entire purchases home!

Peter introduced me to friends of his who had lectured on board the *QE2*, Ken and Aileen Bridgewater. The very British Bridgewaters have lived in Hong Kong for much of their lives and decided to stay after the handover of the British Colony to China in 1997. For them, Hong Kong is home. When I first met Ken and Aileen, however, we had many discussions about the future and whether they would stay. They wanted to stay, but they kept a "bolt hole" as they called it, in England. Now, they are considering selling their "bolt hole" as an act of faith in their belief in the new China.

Aileen Bridgewater had been a well-known radio talk show host in Hong Kong and as such had interviewed countless personalities. "Among these," she told me proudly, "was the Dalai Lama." She is a vivacious and elegant lady and was the model for the character of Gloria Ainsworth in my husband's novel *Two Thousand Years Later*. Her husband, Ken, is a distinguished-looking gentleman who at first exudes typical reserve, but once they had both opened up I realized why Peter liked them so much—they were very warmhearted and most hospitable.

They drove me out to their unique little house in the New Territories, a converted pigery! It is nestled in trees and filled with interesting antiques and books. Sitting in the garden there it was hard to believe that this, too, is a part of bustling Hong Kong. We continued to talk throughout the day. Somehow the subject matter turned to the metaphysical. We each shared stories of deja-vu and seeming memories of having lived before.

The Bridgewaters had arranged for me to be interviewed on Hong Kong Radio to promote a concert planned for the following day and discuss the healing power of music. I traveled by bus to the Government radio station. Prior to my interview, the Radio host spoke to a young woman who was taking groups of artists to Nepal. She described wondrous monasteries in the Himalayas. I wondered if I could then play my Tibetan flute in the interview. It would fit in with the day's theme if I played out my interview to that sound.

My interview started off with the usual questions about my then current tour and the concert life in general. Then, we started in on the healing qualities of music and sound.

"Sound has been used in healing for thousands of years," I commented. "Now this ancient knowledge is coming back. Music therapy is used in many hospitals in America and Europe. Music has always been a very practical tool for me, and especially these days when there is so much stress. It helps a lot to hum a song or even chant a soothing word during a morning meditation." I knew that a Hong Kong audience would at least be familiar with the idea of daily meditation practices.

The interviewer seemed curious. "Could you... maybe demonstrate this singing or chanting for us?" he asked.

"Sure. Why not?" I answered and then proceeded to chant "Hu."

The interviewer looked a little surprised.

"It brings in the sound, the inner music and the light of God," I explained. "It opens the heart to Divine love."

At the end of the interview after my concert had been announced, I played my Tibetan flute. I invited the interviewer to join me by playing my Tibetan bells. This, he seemed to enjoy very much.

The interview ended, I was ushered out of the studio. As I was leaving, my host slipped into the hallway to speak to me off the air. "I'm sorry if I was a little surprised when you sang 'Hu'," he said. "That's my name! You know, I never really liked my name, but maybe now I will take a different attitude toward it." We both went into peels of laughter.

On the evening of that same day, people joined me at the Arts Centre for an eclectic pop and classical concert followed by my lecture on the healing power of music. They responded energetically to the music, but I wasn't sure if they really appreciated the humor. At first they seemed unsure about laughing during a semi-classical performance. I could see them wondering: 'Does she mean to be funny?' Their stiff upper lips began to quiver with laughter. Some

British hang-ups have survived in Hong Kong.

Later that night, still on a high from my performance, I stood alone on my ship overlooking Hong Kong Harbor. I felt the pulse of this vibrant city—so many people, so many sorrows and so many joys. And yet, I felt a profound calmness and peace within myself. We are all inter-connected. We are all one. In every encounter we discover more about our real selves and our purpose here on earth. This is what music has taught me.

It had been a busy day, but I had not had time to shop. I couldn't sail from Hong Kong the next day without shopping at least just for a little while. I went back into the Ocean Terminal and took a cab to Temple Street's night market.

# Chapter Seventeen

# Penguins and Terror del Fuego

S ome of the most engaging animals for which I have ever performed, and certainly the best-educated in proper concert dress, have been South American Penguins. Contrary to popular belief, there are no penguins at the North Pole: their nearest equivalents in the northern hemisphere are probably the puffins. To find penguins in the wild one must travel to the furthest extremities of southern land on our planet. Penguins are found in parts of Australia and New Zealand, they are numerous in southern Chile and Argentina, and naturally abound on the ice shelves of Antarctica. In South America they occupy those parts of Chile and Argentina that were named "Tierra del Fuego" by the Portuguese navigator Magellan, who found a passage through the maze of waterways and islands that make up this southern tip of the Americas. Without the shelter of Magellan's route, ships needed to round Cape Horn, one of the most dangerous areas for sea storms on the planet.

"Tierra del Fuego" literally means the land of fire, and at the time it was an appropriate description for an area of volcanic peaks marking the tip of the Andes mountain chain before it curves through the Southern Ocean bed to re-emerge as that long tail leading into Antarctica. More popularly, therefore, this rugged barren area of South America is known as the "Land of Fire and Ice."

Penguins are very curious creatures. They are not shy. I was amazed how close I could come to these formal gentlemen whom I encountered in Puerto Madryn, and on the Falkland Islands and now at Uschia. Larger than their Australasian cousins, but smaller than the almost human-sized King Penguins of Antarctica, these South American penguins are about knee height.

When I played my flute for the penguins of Uschia, they came walking toward me almost as if I was the "Pied Piper of Hamlyn." They were so like little human beings that I couldn't help talking to them. When they listened to the music they slightly cocked their heads and just opened up their wings in the folds of their 'tail coats' as if to say, "That's nice, play us some more." Play more I did. I performed a whole concert for those penguins! They really loved the music and slowly in little groups they would come out from the surrounding scrub and listen to me as I knelt toward them on the beach. They particularly responded to some of my long, low sounding, ethnic flutes. I don't think, however, that they enthused too much about the piccolo or even my gold flute. The decibels were probably too high for their sensitive little ears. But, where are penguins' ears? Obviously they could hear me playing, but their heads are very sleek and designed for those moments when they dive in to the cold waters to find fish.

However, if you play music with love, it is amazing how nature will respond. I remember an experiment I conducted one time with some fellow musicians. We played music for plants. Over a period of time, calm classical music saw the plants grow towards the speakers. When we changed the music to heavy metal rock, and there is not necessarily anything wrong with heavy metal rock, the plants responded in a negative way, turning their tendrils away from the speakers and even dying at their ends. Do the plants have ears? I don't think so, but they respond to the vibrations of the music. The heavy vibrations of the rock music obviously upset the sensitivity of these particular plants, although there may well be others that would have enthusiastically embraced the music. As a general rule, however, I believe that we are most interconnected with plants and animals through love. If the vibration of the music is loving, their sensitivity will pick this up. The beat is no less music than the melody, but the vibration of the melody seems to be more loving than the vibration of the beat.

And so we come full circle to "Open Your Ears to Love." For us, as human beings, it is our ears that interpret for us the love behind the music. For plants and some animals such as the sea mammals like the dolphins for whom I have also played in Tahiti, it may not literally be their ears that are opened, but the vibration of love, or the life-force that is expressed in the music, is communicated.

Everything is vibration and all vibration can be heard. Music is only vibration. When I play my flutes it is only the vibration of the breath of wind that I blow over the flute hole that creates the sound. This is why at times on stormy days the wind whistles. The wind is not trained as a musician to make notes of sound, but the vibration of the wind in certain circumstances makes whistling sounds that we can detect as music. If we open our ears, or vibratory sensors to the love behind the music, we will experience true music, the music of the spheres that is the music of our life force—the music of God.

The penguins in South America, and the hundreds of other animals for which I have played around the world, have, I hope, felt that interconnection of love that lies behind the music. Sometimes it is easier to express this to innocent animals than in the concert hall, where one is acutely aware that the critics are seated in the front row and your performance is being measured by the opinions and tastes of the different members of the audience. But, apart from that, at least the penguins come dressed in tuxedos!

The evening after I had played for some penguins at Uschia in the heart of "Tierra del Fuego," I experienced "Terror del Fuego."

At 1:15 a.m. our cruise ship was gliding through the Magellan Strait, that inland passage through the southernmost tip of Chile. I had just come in from the deck where the air was unseasonably cold. I sat in the lounge with some of the musicians, singers and dancers of the ship who were relaxing after the last performance of the day. The trombone player suddenly picked up a Brazil nut and held a match under it until it ignited. "Did you know that this one nut will now burn for four hours?" he informed us idly. It seemed an odd subject to bring up.

"Why?" I asked wondering what on earth he was going to say.

"Because it's so oily," he answered.

We all thought about it for a moment. The burning nut smelled gross and was giving off a thick, black smoke. Little did I know this could have been an omen of what was to come that night.

One of the male dancers rebuked the trombonist: "Put it out, man, that stinks!" he shouted. The musician dunked the nut in a water glass and threw it into an ashtray. We moved the conversation on to other topics as we unwound.

Ten minutes later an alarm bell sounded—Seven short rings, and then one long blast. Experienced crewmembers all, we recognized trouble. This was the emergency signal from the Bridge.

"What a crazy time for a fire drill!" I said, almost laughing at the stupidity. "We are all tired, and most of the passengers are surely in bed."

The male dancer went out on deck to see what was going on. As he did so, the voice of the Captain came over the loud speakers: "We have a fire. Everyone must report to their lifeboat station on deck with their life vest on!"

A chill came over me. This was no drill. It was for real! 'A large fire could sink us!' I thought. 'It could destroy the ship.' I ran back down to my cabin four decks below. On my way down, I passed many crewmembers in full lifeboat gear, banging on passengers' doors. "Wake up, wake up! Fire! Fire!" they shouted. "Put your life vest on and report on deck!"

Sleepy passengers emerged with sweaters over nightgowns, dragging their life vests. They looked frightened... panicky.

I reached my cabin door. 'I wonder if I can take a flute with me,' I thought. Then, I wondered which one? Three of my bears were traveling with me. In my mind's eye they seemed to look up at me pathetically as if they sensed some danger. There was Initiate, Bacpac and a new bear, a recent gift from a passenger who as yet had no name. 'Can I take them?' I asked myself. But, the fire drill instructions that we had received when we boarded the ship were explicit: 'Bring nothing with you—just your life vest, and wear warm clothing preferably with some headgear.' I guess people could die trying to fuss with their belongings. I realized that the bears didn't have lifevests. Even the children's lifevests provided on the boat deck would be too big.

So, I put on my thickest sweater and grabbed the life vest from under the bed. I knew a cold wind was blowing outside. 'At least the waters are calm,' I thought, as I struggled to put on my life vest. 'We're in an inland passage and not at sea. But, we're still miles from civilization.' I grabbed my "Visa" card. 'At least I can call my husband if I make it to land—maybe buy a cup of hot tea and a meal if necessary,' I concluded practically. I hugged Initiate Bear and Bacpac, but obediently left them in the cabin along with my precious flutes.

Up on deck, eight-hundred-plus passengers were assembling at their lifeboat stations. Each station had a crewmember to organize one lifeboat. Real fear ran through me as I saw the lifeboats were already released from their davits and ready to be lowered into the water. I knew they didn't do that when the ship was at sea unless it was serious.

"Ladies and gentlemen, there is a fire in the laundry," the female cruise director informed us over the loudspeakers. "We are doing everything possible to extinguish the fire. Please remain calm. Stay at your lifeboat stations. We will keep you informed constantly."

I felt surprisingly calm. 'If this is it,' I said to myself, 'what is my last dream? What should be my last thought... my dying wish?'

I decided to be grateful for my wonderful life. I would like to tell all my loved ones how much I owe this joy to them... that I love them. Peter, my husband came clearly into my mind's eye. I sent him my love. I asked my spiritual guides, whomever they might be, to envelop me in calm joy. I breathed more slowly. I felt kinship with my fellow lifeboat group.

Little by little we all helped each other with small, kind comments to keep our spirits up. Helping another in any situation eases your worry.

Our lifeboat leader was light-hearted. He knew the importance of distracting people from trouble. It proved necessary, to prevent panic. Instead of talking about the fire and what we should do or not do if it got worse, he started playing verbal "Trivial Pursuit" with us. He fired riddles and questions at us as we watched his breath in the night air. Foggily, we tried to answer. Then, he led us into singing:—songs like *Old MacDonald had a Farm* and *Jingle Bells*. It was cold enough to feel like Christmas even though it was mid-summer. Thank God he didn't start up with *Row, Row, Row your Boat*! although a little rowing might have kept us warm.

Pretty soon, our group was smiling and laughing. The music had worked it's magic; we had shifted our focus from the fire. Ironically, we were all now complaining about the bitter cold. An hour or two passed, and our teeth were chattering. Again and again, the Cruise Director came on the loud speaker to tell us things were progressing. But she still didn't let us return to our cabins. The fire had not yet been extinguished and the interior of the ship had filled with asphyxiating smoke.

"We could do with a little of that fire right here," some joker in our group suggested as he blew into his hands. The threat of immediate evacuation seemed to have died down, and such a poorly considered jest was actually now considered funny. People no longer felt their lives to be in danger.

Finally, more progressive news came over the loudspeaker. "Ladies and Gentlemen, the fire is out." There was a cheer from the cold crowd out on the boat deck. The Cruise Director then continued: "We have to ask you to proceed to the Ballroom, as there is still so much smoke in the cabin passageways. Please wait in the Ballroom until there are further announcements."

Immediately, all eight hundred and fifty of us tried to squeeze into the warm ballroom with a seating capacity of six hundred. Members of the crew, still in their lifejackets, brought hot tea and juices to warm us as we jammed together wherever we could find space. We had no idea how long this would last. Passengers, many in nightgowns, began to squat on the floor, putting their life vests down first as a cushion. A few passengers, beginning to sense their own power again after the fright of the event, tried to move out of the ballroom toward the cabin decks. Officers, occasionally taking abuse, swiftly sent them back. Nobody ever seems to understand that asphyxiation from smoke causes most deaths in a fire. The night dragged on until the thin line of dawn broke the horizon.

A kind of euphoria set in. We weren't going to die after all! We had survived! 'Maybe some will die soon,' I thought as I looked at the many old people in their flannel pajamas and night gowns who invariably populate a cruise ship, 'but not tonight. They will dine out on this story.' I was amazed at how calm we all were, with very little complaining. Couples were holding each other endearingly while trying to catch a little sleep. I smiled and helped bring tea to elderly passengers who couldn't move easily around the crowded room.

We camped out in the ballroom for four endless hours. Finally, at about eight in the morning, the announcement we had been waiting for was made. "Ladies and Gentlemen, the smoke has settled. You may return to your cabins. Breakfast service will begin immediately in the restaurant. Today's land tours to see the penguins have been canceled as we are now to remain anchored outside Punta Arenas."

I was so glad that I had gone to see the penguins in Uschia. I went back to my cabin to pack. I was scheduled to leave the ship at this port. I hoped they would let me off in time. What a final night for a cruise!

I was due to fly to Santiago, Chile, and then on to Singapore via Los Angeles and Japan. I had a land concert in Singapore, so I needed to make the connections. Fortunately they let me go. I heard later that our fire-stricken ship stayed in port for two days. The fire had apparently spread into the storage area, and the ship had to wait for more supplies before going on. Among other items, they were totally burned out of toilet paper. It was not an easy place to find sufficient replacement supplies, and the passengers had to stay put for two days making do with Kleenex tissue! But, during the fire and this aftermath, what I call "the world-championship of complaining" had stopped for at least a day. Cruise passengers pay a lot for their voyage and are notoriously finicky. However, everyone I met in the hallways as I dragged my suitcase down to the lowest passenger deck where a tender was to take me ashore, commented on how lucky we were to be alive! How sad that we seem to need a disaster to be reminded how grateful we should be for what we have.

A famous Latin singer was also scheduled to fly with me to Santiago. We had to wait with a customs agent for four or five hours, until they could bring us to the airport. They had taken our passports to be stamped in some other buildings. But, having lived those years in Belo Horizonte in Brazil, I knew this to be business as usual in South America. While we waited in exhaustion, we decided to give a concert to the assembled office.

Why not? As everyone had commented, we were lucky to be alive. The singer said he would start with a couple of popular love songs. He was on a well-known television show in Chile. He popped an accompanying cassette into a small boom box and started to sing with passion and love. As the sound permeated the space, women left their office cubicles and flocked in toward him like bees to honey.

Such is the power of music. The song drew them out of their routines into a magical atmosphere. They screamed and clapped their hands with glee. Then, I took out my flutes and played a Brazilian samba and an Hungarian waltz. Everyone in the room began to dance. From then on the time flew by.

When I looked at my watch, I realized we were about to miss our flight! Just at that moment, the customs agent came running back with our passports and some typical South American red tape forms which nobody ever checks, but which take hours to acquire. Thinking that all was now well, the singer and I boarded our flight for Santiago.

As we flew north, I looked out of the window at the snow-capped mountains and volcanoes of Chile, and thanked that abstract God for my escape from the fire.

From Santiago, I would travel on to Los Angeles and then to Asia. As I went through customs to leave Chile, the South American officials there asked me for the form from Punta Arenas. For the first time I looked at it. It was made out for "Pedro Fandelli," the singer. The agent said to me sarcastically, "Are you Pedro?"

"No!" I affirmed. "There must be some mistake." I looked at the agent and with my knowledge of South America realized that this could take days to straighten out. I tried to explain that obviously the forms we had been handed in Punta Arenas must have been switched. Eventually they bought my story at the cost of a CD and a cassette tape, handy currency that I usually carry with me. They let me board the flight for Los Angeles. 'Phew! Another miracle,' I thought. 'But, I wonder what happened to Pedro Fandelli. Has he managed to explain that he is not Bettine Clemen?'

From Santiago, I flew to Mexico City, a ten-hour flight, and then on to Los Angeles. It was 5 a.m. local time when I arrived. It took a long time to go through US immigration and customs. My next flight was scheduled to leave for Tokyo and Singapore at 10 a.m., so fortunately I had plenty of time. However, I was dead tired after the all night vigil with the fire and a day and night of traveling in South America. Perhaps I was not as alert as I should have been.

I remembered this great bookstore in Los Angeles airport. I headed in that direction to kill time. My luggage was all with me on a rented cart: two suitcases, one flute bag, one bass flute, and my heavy handbag over my shoulder. They weren't checking in baggage for Singapore yet.

I poked around in the bookstore in my exhausted state. There was hardly anybody else browsing at 7 a.m. I drifted toward the Philosophy section and picked up a book by Deepak Chopra called *The Path to Love*. I put my handbag on top of my luggage and began to read. In the corner of my eye I suddenly saw someone walk through the bookstore at a fast clip. I turned my head and my heart stood still. My handbag was gone! I never left it like that before, but I was just so tired.

Now, I was without money, passport, credit cards, Alien Card, which as a German citizen I needed to get back into the US, my tickets to Japan, address books, and cherished childhood pictures including one of Svadi. I broke into a run, trying to find help. "Somebody stole my purse!" I shouted. "Run after him!"

Returning, I talked to the owner of the store, who said he didn't see anything. He offered to call the airport police. Reality then set in. I was in trouble and I had no Identification papers and no money.

Three police officers arrived. They made me fill out forms and took down particulars. They also informed me that four other purses had already been stolen that morning, but this hardly helped me.

After filling out the forms, I went to the Japan Airlines desk to see what could be done about my missing ticket. One of the policemen came with me to explain. Fortunately, they were very understanding and gave me a ticket for the next day. That was fantastic! But, they informed me that if somebody used my stolen ticket; I would have to pay for both tickets. I crossed my fingers and prayed.

By now, I had regained my composure. I tried to think what I should do. I had no money to catch a cab to the German Embassy for a new passport and my address book was gone with all my numbers to call in case of emergency. I started to take inventory. I still had my flutes and my creativity.

'I guess I'll set out a flute case and play for my cab fare,' I thought part in jest and part in desperation. 'Why not?' I started to open my flute bag and saw an old address book inside. My heart leaped with hope. I flipped it open and saw the name of a friend from many years ago who lived right here in Los Angeles. Was there a guardian angel looking over my shoulder, or what?

'Is the phone number still good?' I wondered. 'Can I remember my phone-calling-card number by heart?' I went to a phone bank, but no numbers came into my head. 'Maybe, the familiar pattern of phone keys and the sound of the numbers will just come to me,' I thought. After all, I had dialed my calling card number by rote thousands of times. Fortunately, I must have automatically pressed the right keys, as I really couldn't remember the actual numbers and pin. It worked; I was connected to my friend Denise, who just happened to be home.

"Bettine, I haven't heard from you for years!" she answered excitedly. "I never pick up this phone either, it's just my answering machine line. Something nudged me to pick up and now, there you are."

I told her of my predicament. She immediately said, "Go outside to the curb, and I'll be right there." Fortunately she did not live far from Los Angeles Airport. One of the older policemen led me downstairs and helped me to get my luggage to the curb. He was very kind. He acted like a concerned father. I gave him a CD out of gratitude and on this occasion did not regard it as currency such as had been necessary in South America. He was very appreciative and looked around nervously hoping that no other police officers saw him accept my gift. He did not want it to look like he was accepting a bribe. He was such a sweet man.

As I waited for Denise, I realized that even if you lose something significant, you could concentrate on what you still have, your creativity, and it then creates something better than what you lost! I felt like that about my relationship with this kindly cop.

Denise arrived soon and she immediately drove me to the German Embassy. We chatted away, catching up on our lives. She's such a bright spirit, and had offered to take the day off from her job as a Realtor to drive me around. She told me it was good fortune, as she had wanted to spend some time with me. I started to enjoy the whole experience, even though a thief had invaded my privacy, and even stolen those childhood pictures of me with my horse and my parents. I thought those to be my greatest loss.

At the Embassy, the official to whom I was appointed asked me rather coldly, "How do we know you're German? We need documentation. Do you have your birth certificate?"

'Who travels with their birth certificate,' I wondered remembering for an instant my "bird" certificate trouble on that other ship. "Can't you tell by my accent?" I joked desperately. He was not amused. I switched to German. He was still not convinced.

"We have to call the Chicago Embassy to verify your last passport," he informed me.

Fortunately, I remembered the name of the woman who had helped me get my last passport up in Chicago. It had been two years before, but we had got along rather well and I'd sent her some CD's. If she was still in the Chicago Embassy she just might remember me. I proffered the information to the Los Angeles official.

He told me the verification process would take all day. So Denise and I went out to eat. I started canceling credit cards by phone and stopping my checks. I managed to find a blank check in my luggage. I wrote it out to Denise and she kindly gave me cash in return.

When we returned to the Embassy, they still hadn't managed to reach the woman in Chicago who could verify my passport, but luckily ten minutes before her closing time in Chicago, the Los Angeles authorities did reach her. To their query she immediately answered enthusiastically, "Oh, that German flutist, Bettine! I know her, she's great, and she sent me her music. Give her a passport."

Once again, it was reconfirmed to me that a little generosity to others often pays off. If you give with love, you will receive with love.

Goodwill is the channel of interconnection; it is the life force we call God.

Eight hours after the theft, I now had a new passport, money, a new ticket, had enjoyed a wonderful day with a friend, and had my first good meal since leaving the ship in Punta Arenas. The only thing still missing was my Alien Card from the US, which I desperately needed to get back into the country on my return from Asia. How ironic that I had just used it to be stamped back into the United States before it was stolen. But, there was no time to start the long process of reissue with the US Department of Immigration. I had a booked concert in Singapore and I could still make it there in time if I put off getting the Alien Card. But, it would be a tremendous gamble to leave America without it.

I really had no choice. Not only was this land concert in two days time, but I was scheduled to play a three-month string of concerts throughout Asia. To delay my flight yet another day would create a domino effect on my whole schedule. I had to go. I wondered if maybe I could resolve the alien card problem in India or Japan, where I would have more time? I had no idea. If I didn't resolve it US Immigration might not let me back in to my homeland at the end of my tour. It was my dilemma.

Temporarily dismissing the problem, I stayed overnight with Denise and she dropped me off at the airport early the next morning. We embraced and I promised to stay in better touch. I told her she was my saving angel. Without her, I couldn't have continued my tour.

I settled into the flight, closed my eyes, and felt the wonderful peace that comes from simply being grateful. What a journey! First, the fire on the ship, then a lost pocket book. My thoughts calmed down and I thought of a flight I once boarded from Europe to the USA on which I had met a remarkable human being, my dear friend Jim. I had just boarded the flight and sat down and fastened my seat belt, when I became aware of two stewards carrying in a young-looking very skinny man with glasses. Obviously he was either very ill or paralyzed.

It so happened that this young man sat right across the aisle from me. I felt a strange kinship with him as if I had known him before and pretty soon we started to talk. I found out that he had just visited Germany and that he loved traveling and had a special liking for German culture. He was so vivid and energetic and now, because he was sitting down, nobody would have ever known that he was paralyzed. He told me about his profession. He was a teacher of radio broadcasting and he enthusiastically told me about all his projects. He exuded a courageous spirit and we immediately connected as friends. That flight became a total joy because of this exchange of ideas and energies and I felt no tiredness or boredom. When we landed in the USA, I felt sad that the flight was over as we had enjoyed each other's company so much. We promised to stay friends and since then we have often talked over the phone and I always have been inspired by Jim's strong and loving spirit through which he has completely overcome his physical disability.

A year later, I was touring with Richard in Jim's state, Tennessee, and Jim and I managed to meet again. He came to our concert and afterwards we visited Jim's house and met his wife and children. He told us about his latest projects, which consisted of bringing exchange students from Bulgaria to the States and helping them. He was always helping and inspiring others. For me, he was simply an example of someone who really lived his purpose regardless of any circumstances, and by doing that he was helping and uplifting everyone around him. Here, in the plane, exhausted from my adventures with the thief in Los Angeles, I thought of Jim and our precious friendship and sent him my love.

When I opened my eyes, the man next to me, a quiet, kind-looking Japanese gentleman smiled at me. "Where are you going?" he asked.

I told him about my concert tour and the highlights of my adventures over the past few days. When I finished my story he looked sad, almost as if he was commiserating with me. I asked him, "Where do you live?"

He said, "I am from Kobe, Japan. I was one of the survivors of the recent earthquake, so I know about disaster."

I felt humbled. Everything is relative. He'd apparently lost everything except his wife and son. The rest of his family had died tragically. His house was burned to the ground, except for part of the room where he and his wife had been sleeping. His son was at a friend's house at the time of the quake and at first they hadn't know if their boy had survived.

He told me he took a bicycle and started to look for his son. The city was in chaos. There were fires everywhere and no water to fight them. Scenes of death and destruction were all around. He eventually found his boy trapped under some rubble and got him out alive. The three of them then lived for about eight months in the lobby of a building. There was very little food and water.

"This really transformed my life," the Japanese gentleman commented. "Now, I am much closer to my family. We know what is important—each other, and living each moment to the fullest."

Like Jim, my traveling companion had such gratitude and depth of character. We exchanged addresses and we have corresponded since. Disaster truly can be an opportunity in disguise and as one door closes, another will open if you put your attention on it.

During much of the rest of the flight, when I wasn't sleeping from my exhaustion, I reflected back on my many South American experiences. The continent is such a place of contrasts. Rich live beside poor, great beauty is found beside squalor. The rain forest out from Belo Horizonte had been the inspiration for one of my most successful recordings, but at the same time its senseless rape to satisfy man's greed could be fundamental in the destruction of our planet. I thought again on my travels in those days... the magnificence of Macho Picho, the quiet beauty of mountain villages and towns, the spirit and pace of exciting Rio. More recently on my travels by ship, I had seen Iguassu Falls where mighty rivers meet and crash down into a gorge that is the boundary between Uruguay, Argentina and Brazil. As I thought of the Falls and the strange chipmunk-like animals that inhabit the area, I could hear that haunting music from the film *The Mission*. Much of that movie was shot on location at Iguassu.

I had gone to Iguassu Falls with Peter. It was shortly after we had got engaged and he was still Cruise Director of the *QE2*. The ship was on a cruise around South America and I joined her in Rio de Janeiro to play concerts. It was a memorable voyage; not only because of the magnificent shipboard engagement party that Peter gave for me, but also because of some of the wonderful people we met.

Seated at our table for the full voyage around South America was a marvelous couple from England, although the gentleman was of Scottish ancestry and invariably wore his kilt. Alan and Sheila were relative newly weds compared with most passengers who were contemplating fifty or sixty years of marriage. They had only been married for four years having married relatively late in life. They were middle-aged in their late fifties or early sixties and when they heard about my near-death experience when I was sixteen, Alan shared with us their story.

Alan had experienced a brain tumor and had been close to death. "The only reason that I am alive today is because of Sheila, my wife," he said clearly. "She sat by my bed and when I was hovering in that near-death state, I discovered that I wanted to come back to this life because of her."

I have not often met someone who has enjoyed and appreciated life more than this man. He simply treasured every moment and he was completely in love with Sheila. It is so very valuable to meet someone like that. It makes one think about the preciousness of this life.

One evening when Alan and Sheila came back from a land tour in Puerto Madryn in southern Argentina, Alan told us an exciting story. "Sheila and I were on the bus today when we had an extraordinary experience that we would like to share with you," he announced. "On our bus a very old couple, they must have been in their nineties, was sitting across the aisle from us. The man turned to his wife who apparently had Alzheimer's disease; she never talked or reacted to anything. I couldn't help hearing him say to her, 'Today, sixty years ago we were married.' The woman remained motionless ignoring him and looking straight ahead. After a while, he turned again to her and said, 'The moment when we were married sixty years ago is approaching now. It's close to Noon and we were married at Noon sixty years ago.' Again, the woman showed no response. Sheila and I felt the agony of this man who was trying to get through to his wife. He had obviously loved her very much throughout their marriage, and it was only now that Alzheimer's separated their communication. Sheila leaned across to the woman and very calmly said to her in a loving way, 'We couldn't help but overhear that you were married sixty years ago. We want to congratulate you.' Sheila gently shook the woman's hand and looking directly into her eyes said, 'Congratulations on your anniversary!' At that moment, the muscles in the woman's face started to move. She smiled the most radiant smile and nodded at Sheila. Then, she looked at her husband with that happy expression and mumbled something to him. Then, in front of us all, she kissed him."

While Alan was telling this story, he and Sheila had tears in their eyes. They knew that in opening their hearts to this woman, divine love had flowed through them and gone beyond the blockage of Alzheimer's to ignite the woman's deep love for her husband and their lifetime of memories. Their loving energy had ignited the energy of her soul and given her the power of her inner divinity to overcome the destructive force of temporary disease.

I was very touched by this story, because it showed that this essence which is in all beings and in every atom of the Universe, goes beyond words. It is energy, and it is within us all. It can touch people and be ignited in people independently of their beliefs, religion, cultural background or those barriers that they might have created within themselves. Much of my life, the keys to opening my heart to this Divine love have been contemplation, chanting "Hu," playing my music and the inspiration of nature; but there are other keys as can be seen in the love that Sheila expressed for this stranger. This was true compassion. It is not surprising that Alan fell in love with Sheila. These two had suffered a lot in their lives, but they had found this great love together, and now they were using their love to ignite the invisible essence in others.

Peter and I invited Alan and Sheila to attend the blessing of our marriage in England on July 4th in 1993. It was with great joy as I walked with Peter down the aisle, that I saw them among the congregation. Alan could not be mistaken... he was wearing his kilt.

On that particular journey around South America I met many wonderful people. There was a British explorer who had crossed the continent through the rain forests of Brazil by jeep. Robin Hanbury-Tennison had lived with the Yamamimi Indians for six months and shared the experience. These Indians of the upper Amazon live a very simple and spiritual life. They share everything and have not yet discovered money. Robin experienced and shared the natural harmony that these people still have. Then, there was a lady who was teaching relief from stress. Actually, some passengers who enjoyed her told me that they were just 'off to the lecture of the lady who teaches stress.' I couldn't help myself from correcting them. "She's not teaching stress," I said, "She's supposed to be teaching relief from stress." However, on the voyage she continued to be described by most people as the "Stress" lady! But, one of my greatest joys was meeting the clergy with whom Peter was sharing his ministry of love on that voyage. There was Father D'Arcy, a lovely man from Ireland who probably had never read a Theological book since Seminary, who loved his wee drop of whiskey, but who simply radiated love. Father D'Arcy is dead now, but the fact that he was so loved by the crew of the *QE2* was fair testimony of the man's inner love. Peter also introduced me to one of his greatest spiritual friends, an Anglican Archdeacon Emeritus of New York. Bob Willing has known his share of suffering from a difficult fight with cancer to a troublesome divorce in an ecclesiastical establishment that offered little support or sympathy, but like Father D'Arcy, Bob is a man of enormous love and human tolerance. I was so happy that he could be present when Peter and I were married in that ceremony in the garage of my dome house. Bob read from Gibran's *The Prophet*. Peter has a special bond with this man in which I feel I now share.

I was reminded of something my husband said to me about his days as a Cruise Director. He told me that each day he prayed that his divine light might shine from him to inspire the divinity within others. He used to read a poem at the beginning of every voyage when he introduced his staff. It is a well-known but anonymous poem:

'A smile costs nothing, but gives much.
It enriches those who receive, without making poorer
    those who give.
It takes but a moment, but the memory of it sometimes lasts forever.
None is so rich and mighty that he can get along without it,
And none is so poor that he can not be made rich by it.
A smile creates happiness in the home, fosters goodwill in business,
And is the countersign of friendship.
It brings rest to the weary, cheer to the discouraged,
    sunshine to the sad,
And is nature's best antidote for trouble.
Yet it cannot be bought, begged, borrowed or stolen,
For it is something that is of no value to anyone
    until it is given away.
Some people are too tired to give you a smile;
    give them one of yours,
As none needs a smile so much as he who has no more to give.'

So, you see, no words are really needed. You don't have to explain about this essence. It's in all of us and it's contagious. It can be experienced because it is interconnected with all life. It can be awakened in all life whether animal, plant or human. It is even present in the inanimate objects, and in the gasses and boundless energy from which we are formed.

After twenty hours of flying and reflecting on these things, I arrived in Singapore. My friend picked me up and took me to the Shangri-La Hotel. It felt like Shangri-La as I sank into the luxury of a hot bath, feeling like I had come home from a war. The concert went well, and while in Singapore I managed to get another visa to enter India. Eventually, in London, England, I got that all important letter from the United States Embassy acknowledging that I had lost my Alien

Card when my purse had been stolen in Los Angeles nearly three months before. I sailed from Southampton, England on the *QE2* for that final leg home to the USA. They indeed let me back into the States with that letter, and I had a few weeks to reflect and rest.

I felt as if the harvest had come in. I had been showered with wondrous and colorful experiences and had fully felt the power of creativity. I had so totally experienced the many moments of this leg of my life's journey and had witnessed the joy of learning from the whole creation be it people, animals, plants or the silence. As source we can all awaken in each other. What we see is various aspects of ourselves. We are it. It is up to us.

We can open our ears to love with deliberate intention. We can indeed find inner peace; we can let go of the blockages and walls that keep us from standing in our own power... our awareness—that which we are that is beyond time and space.

Open your ears to love!

## FOREVER

*Suns rise and set,*
*Moons sail in and out,*
*We change our form,*
*Yet, where is forever?*
*In the music of the wind it sings,*
*In the eyes of a child it lives,*
*In the fragrance of a rose it dreams,*
*Forever is the love that dwells within.*

*–Bettine*

# *Epilogue*

O n my Life's journey I have experienced many viewpoint shifts. Quite often, after I had embraced a certain belief or belief system and considered it to be the highest and ultimate truth, it changed for me and faded away losing its power to satisfy my quest to truly know who I am and where I am going. The search then continued. Again, the carpet on which I was traveling was pulled away from under me and I had to face the nothingness—no absolute answers. Now, as I look back, I consider this process to have been a blessing and I realize that none other than myself created it that way. All the different paths and ways were helpful and brought me to where I am now. But, the now is all there is. Now, I believe that there is no ultimate truth. We are crafting and creating our experiences constantly. We are eternal, infinite energy, and we are not the creations with whom we have identified. I had touched that essence for the first time in this life in my car accident. I had pursued it and reexperienced it in my years of practicing meditation, soul travel, and being a member and practitioner of Eckankar. But, I was still living in an old paradigm, the paradigm of some higher or "other" force or source running my life.

Recently, I came across a course called "Avatar," which is based upon the simple concept that your beliefs will cause you to create or attract the experiences that you call your life. It teaches total self-responsibility and provides the tools through which we can awaken in our ability to explore our own consciousness and to experience the deep peace that underlies it.

My whole life has changed dramatically. I came to realize how much certain beliefs I had treasured and considered, were just that—

beliefs. I also realized how much some of them had been holding me back. I finally learned to make that connection, and to deliberately create and change my belief structure and therefore my experiences.

Now, I feel life is an exploration, and my travels around the world are a symbol of my life's explorations and adventures. I am grateful for all the encounters and teachings of the past. I send my love to all of them. But, I know that true expansion is infinite and eternal. There is no end... there is no absolute truth. What is the Divine to me is that infinite expansive quality that drives everyone and everything. Mentally, it is the never ceasing desire for me to explore more of all there is within me.

I believe that the answers are inside of us and that following someone else's answers does not necessarily bring us closer to our truth. For me, love is still a very real force. I grew through love—through joy and also through some pain... through living fully. There is no escape from life, only understanding and awareness.

As I am looking for words that could express my innermost thoughts about this life's journey, the letter I received from that eight-year-old boy comes into my mind again. The post scriptum that he had scribbled down for me in crooked letters says it all in just a few words:

*Life is a Song for the Heart that is Free*

This simple saying indicates that when our heart is free of all our self-made limitations, then we can compose, create and sing our very own song and create our own symphony of life. All the notes and melodies will be of our own creation.

We are in our essence the creating energy that is divine and is co-creating with all there is. If we take total responsibility for everything in our lives, we can then change our lives and put into action all we learned from all of our life experiences. The song we sing includes all the different shades of experiences, all the notes, all the melodies, whether in a major or minor key, they all are part of our composition.

I have spent many years searching for the real meaning of life and for the "Absolute Truth," and even though I sincerely embraced several paradigms, such as "Life is a school for Soul," or "Life is a Spiritual Experience," as soon as I grew comfortable with any of these explanations and belief systems, I somehow got booted out of them by my own curiosity for new explorations. I feel only gratitude toward the paths and spiritual teachers that have helped me and guided me on this journey, but in the end I believe that we are our own Masters. The truth is constantly evolving and reshaping through our own creative powers. We are 'infinite divine energy having a human experience' rather than 'humans looking and searching for that infinite source.' The answers, if there are any, all lie within us.

When we are free inside... free to access our creative power, and uncluttered with disabilitating beliefs and worrying thoughts about the past or the future, then we can sing freely and create a lifesong filled with love, harmony and limitless joy. All the many books I have read were inspiring, and some of them came close to my own inner feelings about life. None, however, expressed the essence of life as well as this eight-year-old boy.

Yes, David, life is a song when the heart is free, and by thanking you with all my heart, I thank all the thousands of people along with the animals and plants who have helped me to remember this. May your life be a song, and may you always know in your heart that you can choose the song you want to sing in this life, and that it can also be a song of love!

Open your heart, ears and eyes, and your whole being to the infinite love that you are!

*"When you adopt the viewpoint that there is nothing that exists that is not part of you, that there is no one who exists who is not part of you, that any judgment you make is self-judgment, that any criticism you level is self-criticism, you will wisely extend to yourself an unconditional love that will be the light of your world."*

–Harry Palmer—*Author of the Avatar materials*

*From the poems of Rumi*

*The clear bead at the center changes everything.*
*There are no edges to my loving now.*
*I've heard it said, there's a window*
*that opens from one mind to another.*
*But if there's no wall, there's no need*
*for fitting the window, or the latch.*

*–Rumi*

# Appendix A

# Exercises

I believe joy and love are the highest contributions we can make to life. Here are some of my favorite techniques to bring more joy and more love into your life with music. Feel free to modify them to fit your own needs in the moment.

## *Toning:*

This is a simple exercise in which you use your voice to harmonize yourself with life. But, you can't be bashful. If you're not used to singing or talking out loud like my crazy musician friends and me it helps to be alone the first time you try this exercise. It is one of the fastest methods I know to get in tune, or balance, physically, mentally, and spiritually.

Sit down and straighten your back as you draw in a deep breath. Look to the inner screen of your mind, and imagine a moment that brought you great happiness. It can be as simple as greeting a dog on the street, or holding your child on your lap. With this image in mind, gently begin to sing out loud. You can pick any word or sound that seems uplifting to you. It can be a vowel sound, like "oo" or a word or name of a loved one, or a word considered sacred by many such as

"Hu," an ancient name for God. Westerners are very resistant to making such random sounds, but they are a very inborn, natural part of ourselves. The first thing a baby does is scream, or make a "joyful noise."

Experiment with singing your sound at various pitches up and down the musical scale. Try placing your hand over your chest. Which notes resonate (make your hand vibrate) the most? Sing those over and over again, drawing out the sound with each breath as you relax and concentrate on the inner screen of your mind. Now let your voice drift down into the deeper registers as you gently exhale each note.

It might take a little practice, but after awhile, relaxation will come creeping in. You might even begin to see some light filtering in to the screen of your mind, or hear a humming or an inner melody. Sing it out loud. This is the audible life stream, the life force that connects us to all life.

By using your voice, you are tuning yourself as an instrument for life. I believe this is why moaning or keening is a time-honored way to get through pain. It expresses our innermost feelings, but don't confine it to sadness. Why not express your joy, too? Don't be afraid to let all your feelings out as you sing—show happiness, sadness and everything in between in the notes of your music. Exhale any tension, and keep resonating with the notes.

When your song ends, listen to the sound current ringing in your ears, or move into gentle meditation. The singing is very centering. As you finish, invite the melodies of life to move through you for the rest of the day. Watch as all kinds of new people and situations respond to this higher intent! You are truly a song, and life will reflect your melody back to you.

## *Music for Health:*

The key to this exercise is to first find some music that energizes your soul. Keep in mind that dancing to wild rock beats refreshes some people, while others are uplifted by calm, classical reveries.

Try experimenting with music of your choice. Use the form included to record how it affects you physically, emotionally, mentally, and spiritually. Enter the music, and let it touch the core of your being. Just five minutes of true, participatory listening can brighten your whole day.

If you want to be more scientific about this, note how each musical piece affects your heart rate, either to slow it down or speed it up. Your breathing will be changed, your blood pressure will rise or fall, and your muscle tension will slacken or tighten.

With experimentation, you'll find that to rev yourself up, you need a faster beat. If you need to relax, slower music will help your shoulders to drop from around your ears, and make you exhale all that stress.

If you want to heal or change your outlook, try a technique called "pacing." The idea is not to try to force yourself to be "happy" when you're sad. In other words, don't try to get out of a depression by listening to Souza marches. Instead, pick out a favorite blues album. Why? Because it will echo and express how you feel right in this moment.

That is important—to express and feel the truth of NOW. Put on some sad music and be completely in the moment. Let the music carry all your feelings as you drift or even sob along with the melody.

Now, notice your feelings at the end. Are you feeling a bit more relaxed? Then "pace" yourself with a piece that is just a bit more upbeat. Music can uplift you much more easily if you gradually move yourself up and out of the blues. Gentle movement is the most effective.

This is a good tip to keep in mind even on a casual basis. When you first come home from work all tired and grumpy, put the CD player to work. Pick something bluesy. This will match or "pace" your mood after driving in traffic. Then, gradually work your way to more relaxing or happy tunes, until you feel soothed and ready to unwind for the rest of the evening.

## *You are a Song:*

This is a more advanced technique worth trying. Find a quiet place in your home or out in nature, somewhere where you will be undisturbed for a few minutes. Sit or lie down, take a few deep breaths, and relax. Just be in silence for a few moments. Let the silence fill your ears until they are humming with a subtle ringing.

Now, using your imagination, begin to listen to the little sounds around you—the car going by, the hum of the refrigerator, the bird singing, the dog barking. Let these incidental noises join in as you begin to imagine a simple melody. Pretend it is the most wonderful song and sound you can imagine. Is it a violin, a flute, a piano, a symphony or some unearthly sound? A quick or slow melody? Visualize the notes going up and down, the shape your melody creates as it speaks to you. Don't worry if you can't actually hear music. Just go with the idea of it filling your world.

Don't get discouraged, this technique takes practice. But, many times people will actually report that their inner ears are filled with a unique song. Others move on to a meditative state, which refreshes their mind. Sometimes an insight comes, or a little "ah ha!" that could make your day easier. The music could be something you've heard before or something completely original. Sometimes it stays the same for days, or changes six times in as many minutes. Some people have their own "theme song" that seems to express who they are or just how they feel.

The whole point is to believe you are music, and to fall in love with this music inside you. Each day, try to go back to this melody you love. As I mentioned, it can change or stay the same. Whatever it is, is a reflection of you, the song that you are right now. Embrace it and become one with it. Dance to the rhythm of this song for the rest of your day.

## *"Natural" Stress Buster:*

If you're feeling worried, or your mind is racing over all you have to accomplish, try this exercise. Go outside and spend at least fifteen to twenty minutes with the trees, the grass, and the plants. Even one city tree works for this exercise. Let your whole attention be absorbed by the sights and sounds around you.

Let your mind calm itself. Live completely in the moment. Don't let any worry creep in from the past or about the future. Most tension comes from what has already happened or worrying about what will happen. But, don't try to prevent tension, just immerse yourself in the peace of nature, the natural music of life that is flowing through "your" tree.

Now, I know it sounds silly, but ask the tree for a song, or a bit of advice. What does it have to say or sing to you? Laugh out loud if it seems absurd, but don't totally dismiss the possibility. What if the tree really had a gift for you? What would it be? Mere receptivity is all that counts. It will displace your fears, worries, and limitations. Looking at a natural melody in the form of a tree relaxes your mind, so your true self can emerge.

## Focusing Exercise:

When you're feeling unfocused, sluggish, spacey, or down, try this technique. Put on any rhythmical or wild piece. Make sure it has a strong bass and drum beat. Now drop your inhibitions and move wildly with it. Don't be judgmental. Just move to the music. Imagine you're a child again, just exploring and experiencing the music with your body.

See how the movement shifts your energy? It seems to burn off your foggy mood and energize you to be focused and joyful. As a child you are naturally in this state of wonder and joy. Everything is newly discovered. Later in life you lose this ability, but it's still in you.

You can recreate every moment so life becomes an adventure again. Hold this simple viewpoint throughout the day. Think of yourself as an explorer of life, rather than an endurer or sufferer. Suffering is optional in life! At any given moment, you can recreate or remake your past and most importantly in this moment. Let go of pain and worry to embrace the joy of life.

## A Sound Bath:

Choose a favorite piece of music that seems to relax you. It can be Celtic melodies, classical music, or soft jazz. Now, lie smack in the middle of the floor on your back. (These exercises do work on your inhibitions, don't they?) Now, take a few deep breaths. Let yourself sink into the sound and into the floor at the same time. Imagine the sound massaging every cell of your being. Let it wash through you like a cleansing rain, touching and cleansing your body, thoughts, and emotions.

Put your attention lightly on the screen of your mind. Visualize the sound in the form of light. Pick your favorite color. Expand it into other colors, and eventually into pure gold, and then bright, white light.

Bathe in this sound become light. Let it circulate for a few minutes inside and around your body. You will be filled with energy.

# *Appendix B*

# *Book List*

## *Music and Healing*

A Soprano on her Head – Eloise Ristad
The Listening Book – W.A. Mathieu
Sound Medicine – Laeh Maggie Garfield
The Secret Power of Music – David Tame
The Healing Energies of Music – Hal. A. Lingerman
Tuning the Human Instrument – Dr. Stephen Halpern
Soundhealth – Dr. Stephen Halpern
Through Music to the Self – Peter Michael Hamel
'Nada Brahma' - The World is Sound – Joachim Ernst Berendt
The Third Ear – Joachim Ernst Berendt
The Flute of God – Paul Twitchell
The Conscious Ear – Alfred A. Tomatis
The Silent Pulse – George Leonard
Music and Miracles – Don Campbell
Music—Its Secret Influence through the Ages – Cyril Scott
The Life Energy in Music (3 Vols.) – John Diamond, M.D.
Return to Harmony – Nicole La Voie

## *Health and Healing*

You can heal your Life – Louise L. Hay

The Power of the Mind to Heal – Joan Borysenko, Ph.D.
Guilt is the Teacher; Love is the Lesson – Joan Borysenko, Ph.D.
Fire in the Soul – Joan Borysenko, Ph.D.
Hands of Light – Barbara Ann Brennan
Ageless body, Timeless Mind – Deepak Chopra
Quantum Healing – Deepak Chopra
The Five Tibetans – Christopher S. Kilham
New Cells, New Bodies, New Life! – Virginia Essene
Stillness is the Way – Barry Long
Breathing, Expanding your Power & Energy – Michael Sky
The Twelve Stages of Healing – Dr. Donald M. Epstein
Rebirthing in the New Age – Leonard Orr and Sondra Ray
Drinking the Divine – Sondra Ray
Natural Health, Natural Medicine – Andrew Weil, M.D.
Spontaneous Healing – Andrew Weil, M.D.
Super-Learning – Sheila Ostrander & Lynn Schroeder
Inner Communion – Sondra Ray
Celebration of Breath – Sondra Ray

## *Spirituality and Philosophy*

Everyday Soul – Bradford Keeney, Ph.D.
Dare to be yourself – Alan Cohen
Living Deliberately – Harry Palmer
A Modern Prophet
     Answers your Key Questions about Life – Harold Klemp
Answers – Mother Meera
The Presence of God – Brother Lawrence
The Seven Spiritual Laws of Success – Deepak Chopra
You'll see it when you believe it – Wayne Dyer
The Starseed Transmissions – Ken Carey
Why Christianity must Change or Die – Bishop John Shelby Spong
The Coming of the Cosmic Christ – Matthew Fox
Conversations with God Book One – Donald Neale Walshe
Conversations with God Book Two – Donald Neale Walshe
The Path to Love – Deepak Chopra
The Spiritual Exercises of ECK – Harold Klemp
Many Masters, many Lives – Brian Weiss, Ph.D.
Only Love is Real – Brian Weiss, Ph.D.

Original Blessing – Matthew Fox
The Messengers – Julia Ingram and G.W. Hardin
Honest to God – John A.T. Robinson
Experiences with Invisible Realities – John Jensen
The Tenth Insight – James Redfield
Future Diary – Mark Victor Hansen
Sufism – Hazrat Inayat Khan
A Cup of Tea – Osho
I celebrate Myself – Osho
Surfing the Himalayas – Frederick Lenz
The Tapestry of Light – Susan Drew
Starchildren – Jenny Ranles
The Hunger of Eve – Barbara Marx Hubbard
The Spiritual Journey – Anne Bancroft
Healing our World, The other Piece of the Puzzle – Dr. Mary J.
    Ruwart
My Master is my Self – Andrew Cohen
The Robot's Rebellion – David Icke
And the Truth shall set you Free – David Icke
I am me, I am Free – David Icke
Hidden Journey – Andrew Harvey
The Way of Passion, A Celebration of Rumi – Andrew Harvey
Dialogues with a Modern Mystic – Andrew Harvey & Mark
    Matousek
A Vision of an Empty Cross – Peter Longley
Discovering Life's Trails, Adventures in Living – Tom Dennard
In the Company of ECK Masters – Phil Morimitsu
Life and Teaching of the Masters of the Far East – Baird T. Spalding
Earth, Pleiadian Keys to the Living Library – Barbara Marciniak
Bridges to Heaven – Jonathan Robinson
Awaken the Gods – Chuck Spezzano Ph.D.
Every Moment's a Miracle – Leo Drioli
The Infinite Voyage – Martin Ernst-Wolfgang Luther
Dare to Win – Jack Canfield and Mark Victor Hansen
Chicken Soup for the Soul – Jack Canfield and Mark Victor Hansen
The Perennial Philosophy – Aldous Huxley
Zen: The Quantum Leap from Mind to No-Mind – Osho
The Tantra Experience—Osho

You are the Key – Shaun de Warren

35 Golden Keys to Who you are and Why you are here – Linda C.
   Anderson

Anyone can see the Light – Dianne Morrissey

The Wind is my Mother – Bear Heart

## Spiritual Poetry

Sonnets to Orpheus – Rainer Maria Rilke

Say I am You – Rumi

Like This – Rumi

Unseen Rain – Rumi

Mystical poems – Kabir

Stranger by the River – Paul Twitchell

My Love for You – Thomas Drayton

Speaking Flame – Andrew Harvey

Music of Soul – Thomas Drayton

## Near Death Experiences

The Tibetan Book of Living and Dying – Sugyal Rinpoche

Life after Death – Raymond Moody

Coming Back – Raymond Moody

Heading Toward Omega – Kenneth Ring, Ph.D.

Lessons from the Light – Kenneth Ring Ph.D.

Saved by the Light – Dannion Brinkley

At Peace in the Light – Dannion Brinkley

Closer to the Light – Melvin Morse, M.D.

Life Before Life – Helen Wambach

## Novels

Two Thousand Years Later – Peter Longley

Legacy of a Star – Peter Longley

Beyond the Olive Grove – Peter Longley

The Mist of God – Peter Longley

The Celestine Prophecy – James Redfield

Illusions – Richard Bach

Jonathon Livingston Seagull – Richard Bach

The Tiger's Fang – Paul Twitchell

Contact – Carl Sagan

Mutant Message from Down Under – Marlo Morgan
2150 AD. – Thea Alexander
I Remember Union – Flo Calhoun
Out on a Limb – Shirley McLaine
The Golden Dream – Heather Hughes-Calero
Buzzards Roost – Tom Dennard

## Animals

Animal Speak – Ted Andrews
Journey to the Center of Creation – Ilona Selke
Kinship with all Life – J. Allen Boone

## Animal Newsletter

Angel Animals® – Allen and Linda Anderson
(For a Free Copy call 1-888-925-3309)

## Science

The Dragons of Eden – Carl Sagan
The Holographic Universe – Michael Talbot
The Silent Pulse – George Leonard
The Holographic Paradigm and other Paradoxes – Ken Wilber
Regaining Wholeness Through the Subtle Dimensions – Don Paris

# About the Author

*"Music speaks directly to the heart and soul of the listener,*
*and can by-pass all differences of language, race and culture.*
*It truly is the universal language of the world. It can uplift*
*the listener's mind, body and spirit."*

*– Bettine*

B ettine is a world-renowned solo flautist and international recording artist. Her concerts featuring many different flutes bring together the varied aspects of her career combining the classics, popular music, light jazz and original compositions. Her music has a profound effect on all her audiences regardless of age or venue, which is a reflection of her innovative creative ability to touch humanity.

Born in Bavaria, Bettine gained her Masters degree at the Academy of Music in Munich. Among her teachers were Aurele Nicolet, James Galway, Julius Baker and Peter-Lukas Graf. Early in her career, Bettine had many acclaimed performances with prestigious orchestras including the Munich Bach Orchestra, the Prague Radio Orchestra and the Mozarteum Orchestra of Salzburg. In 1978, she became solo flautist of the Belo Horizonte Symphony in Brazil. Bettine's appreciation of the Amazon rainforest served as quiet inspiration for her successful recording project *Love Song to a Planet* in collaboration with well-known Celtic harpist Kim Robertson.

Later Bettine relocated to the United States performing with the San Francisco Bach Society and embarking on a career touring for Columbia Artistes. Together with Classical guitarist Richard Patterson she played over 170 concerts in the United States and recorded four more CD's. Their Christmas album, *An Angel's Noel*, was nominated as the best Christmas recording of 1991 and has sold nearly 300,000 copies worldwide to date.

Her exhilarating solo concerts take her to the far reaches of the world including Europe, all of Asia and Australia with invitations to perform in such prestigious venues as the Festival Hall and Royal Albert Hall in London as well as the Lincoln Center in New York. She was also one of the first western musicians officially invited by the Chinese government to perform concerts and teach master classes in Shanghai and Beijing.

Among Bettine's more recent recordings are *Forever* with members of the St. Paul Chamber Orchestra, *Open Your Ears to Love*, a compilation of hits culled from over fifteen years of recording, and an album of international folk songs entitled *Echoes of Life*.

Bettine is involved in spectacular multi-media presentations including *Love Song from Planet Earth* in collaboration with world famous Canadian photographer Courtney Milne incorporating solo flute with full orchestra and stunning visual images, which was premiered with the Saskatoon Symphony to great acclaim.

In between engagements, Bettine is much sought after as a headliner artist on international luxury cruise ships and has completed this book, *Open Your Ears to Love*, expressing her philosophy of music and life and incorporating many of her traveling experiences. She lives in Minnesota and Georgia with her husband Peter Longley, author of the unusual spiritual travel adventure *Two Thousand Years Later*.

For many years Bettine has advocated and practiced the healing power of music, lecturing and presenting workshops on this fascinating subject. She is a featured mainstay at conferences and expositions around the world. As a licensed 'Avatar' master she delivers 'Avatar' courses all over the world teaching tools of self-empowerment. It has always been her heartfelt belief that music is for all ages and can be a tool to wholeness and wellbeing.

# Catalog of Recordings

All Recordings are available through
*Joy of Music*

Bettine Clemen
P.O. Box 204
Seymour, MO 65746 USA

E-Mail: bettine@joyofmusic.com

Website: www.joyofmusic.com

## CD's
**Independent Label (All listed at $15.00 + $ 3.00 post and packing)**
*Echoes of Life (Bettine Clemen-Flutes & Richard Patterson-Guitar)*
*Open Your Ears to Love (Bettine Clemen-Flutes)*

**Sugo Recordings (All listed at $15.00 + $3.00 post and packing)**
(Call 1-800-927 SUGO for local sales information)
*Forever (Bettine Clemen-Flutes & Richard Patterson-Guitar)*
*An Angel's Noel (Bettine Clemen-Flutes & Richard Patterson-Guitar)*
*Past, Present & Future (Bettine Clemen-Flutes & Richard Patterson-
    Guitar)*
*Classical Offering (Bettine Clemen-Flutes & Richard Patterson-Guitar)*

**Invincible Recordings (Listed at $15.00 + $3.00 post and packing)**
*Love Song to a Planet (Bettine Clemen-Flutes & Kim Robertson-Celtic
    Harp)*

# CASSETTES
## Independent Label (All listed at $10.00 + $2.00 post and packing)
*Dancing in Sound (Bettine Clemen Ware)*
*Sunny Days (Bettine Clemen Ware-Flutes & Richard Lawrence-Violin)*
*Inside Passage (Bettine Clemen Ware-Flutes & Richard Patterson-Guitar)*
*Images (Bettine Clemen Ware-Flute & Richard Patterson-Guitar)*
*Harpourri (Bettine Clemen Ware-Flute & Andrea Stern-Harp)*
*Sunrise (Bettine Clemen Ware-Flute & Merrill Davis-Piano)*
*On Eagle's Wings Vol:I (Bettine Clemen Ware-Flutes & Elizabeth Turrell-Harp)*
*On Eagle's Wings Vol:II (Bettine Clemen Ware-Flutes & Elizabeth Turrell-Harp)*
*Live in Concert (Bettine Clemen Ware-Flute, Elizabeth Turrell-Harp & the Palo Alto Chamber Orchestra)*
*Concertino in D—J.M. Sperger & Duo for Flute and Double Bass-Robert Le Blanc (Bettine Clemen-Flute & the Prague Radio Chamber Orchestra)*
*Blue Faience Hippopotamus (Bettine Clemen Ware-Flutes & Richard Lawrence-Violin)*

## Sugo Recordings (All Listed at $10.00 + $ 2.00 post and packing)
(Call 1-800-927 SUGO for local sales information)
*Forever (Bettine Clemen-Flutes & Richard Patterson-Guitar)*
*Classical Offering (Bettine Clemen-Flutes & Richard Patterson-Guitar)*
*An Angel's Noel (Bettine Clemen-Flutes & Richard Patterson-Guitar)*
*Past, Present & Future (Bettine Clemen-Flutes & Richard Patterson-Guitar)*

## Invincible Recordings (Listed at $10.00 + $2.00 post and packing)
*Love Song to a Planet (Bettine Clemen-Flutes & Kim Robertson-Celtic Harp)*

## TO ORDER

Please send check or Money Order made out to *Joy of Music* and including post and packing to the following address:

Bettine Clemen                          *55345*
P.O. Box 204
Seymour, MO  65746
E-Mail: bettine@joyofmusic.com
Website: www.joyofmusic.com

*Music!*
*Rivers of sound embracing the earth,*
*igniting the soul in a love song to life.*
*Forests, eagles, crickets and wolves,*
*bring all your sounds!*
*Let us dance through the night!*
*Oceans, stars, suns and moons,*
*Sing with us now in currents of light.*

*–Bettine*

# Avatar

## *The Art of Living Deliberately*

Avatar is a course based upon the simple concept that your beliefs will cause you to create or attract the experiences that you call your life.

When you change what you believe, you change your life. Avatar is an awakening of your ability to explore your own consciousness and to experience the deep peace that underlies it.

*The Avatar Course is in three sections:*

Section 1 Resurfacing® Two-Day Workshop
Section 11 & 111: The Avatar Course

Courses are available throughout the year in varying locations

**If you would like to discover more about future Avatar courses**

**Please call**

## Bettine Clemen

### Avatar Master and Wizard

Bettine Clemen
P.O. Box 204
Seymour, MO 65746
E-Mail: bettine@joyofmusic.com
Website: www.joyofmusic.com